# REVISE EDEXCEL GCSE
# Mathematics
## Higher

# GUIDED REVISION WORKBOOK

Series Consultant: Harry Smith

Author: Fiona Harris and Eleanor Jones

- - - - - - - - - - - - - - - - - - - - - - - - - - - - - - - - - - - - - - - - - - - - - - - -

## Notes from the publisher

While the publishers have made every attempt to ensure that advice on the qualification and its assessment is accurate, the official specification and associated assessment guidance materials are the only authoritative source of information and should always be referred to for definitive guidance.

Pearson examiners have not contributed to any sections in this resource relevant to examination papers for which they have responsibility.

---

**For the full range of Pearson revision titles across KS2, KS3, GCSE, Functional Skills, AS/A Level and BTEC visit:**
www.pearsonschools.co.uk/revise

---

**Question difficulty**
Look at this scale next to each exam-style question. It tells you how difficult the question is.

---

# Contents

**A small bit of small print**
Edexcel publishes Sample
Assessment Material and the
Specification on its website. This is
the official content and this book
should be used in conjunction with
it. The questions in this book have
been written to help you practise
what you have learned in your
revision. Remember: the real exam
questions may not look like this.

# Factors and primes

**1** Here is a list of numbers:

    2    4    5    8    10    12    21

From this list, write down

(a) a square number .......4...... **(1 mark)**   (b) a prime number ......2........ **(1 mark)**

(c) a multiple of 6 ........12........ **(1 mark)**   (d) a factor of 15 ......10........ **(1 mark)**

**2** (a) Write 90 as a product of its prime factors.

| Product means 'times'. |

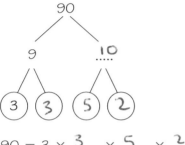

Use a factor tree. Circle factors when they are prime – these are at the end of the branches.

$90 = 3 \times \underline{3} \times \underline{5} \times \underline{2}$

$= 3^2 \times \underline{5} \times \underline{2}$ **(2 marks)**

(b) Write 120 as a product of its prime factors.

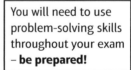 

$120 = \underline{5 \times 2^2 \times 3^2}$ **(2 marks)**

**3** Find the HCF and LCM of 90 and 120.

**PROBLEM SOLVED!**

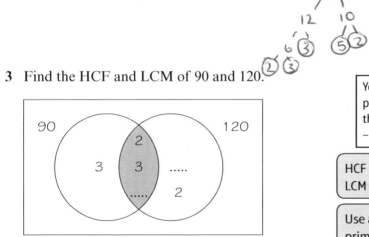

You will need to use problem-solving skills throughout your exam – **be prepared!**

HCF is Highest Common Factor. LCM is Lowest Common Multiple.

Use a Venn diagram to show the prime factors of 90 and 120.

HCF = 2 × 3 × ...... = ......

The HCF is the product of the prime factors in the intersection. **(2 marks)**

LCM = 3 × 2 × 3 × ...... × ...... × 2 = ......

The LCM is the product of all the prime factors in the union. **(3 marks)**

**4** Find the LCM and HCF of 48 and 60.

**PROBLEM SOLVED!**

You will need to use problem-solving skills throughout your exam – **be prepared!**

HCF = ........    LCM = ........

**(3 marks)**

# Indices 1

**1** Write as a single power of 3

(a) $3 \times 3 \times 3 \times 3 =$

.............................

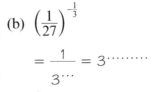
How many times is 3 multiplied by itself? This gives you the index.

(b) $\left(\dfrac{1}{27}\right)^{-\frac{1}{3}}$

$= \dfrac{1}{3^{\cdots}} = 3^{\cdots\cdots}$

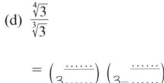
Remember, $\dfrac{1}{a} = a^{-1}$. What power of 3 do you have in the denominator?

(c) $\sqrt[4]{3^8}$

$= \dfrac{3^{\cdots}}{3^{\cdots}} = 3^{\cdots - \cdots} =$

First write as a fraction, then subtract indices.

(d) $\dfrac{\sqrt[4]{3}}{\sqrt[3]{3}}$

$= \left(3^{\frac{\cdots\cdots}{\cdots\cdots}}\right)\left(3^{-\frac{\cdots\cdots}{\cdots\cdots}}\right)$

$= \dots\dots\dots\dots\dots\dots$

**2** (a) Simplify

(i) $x^3 \times x^5 = x^{3+5} = x^{\cdots}$ **(1 mark)**

(ii) $x^2 \times x^7 = x^{\cdots}$ **(1 mark)**

(b) Simplify

(i) $x^7 \div x^3 = x^{7-3} = x^{\cdots}$ **(1 mark)**

(ii) $x^8 \div x^2 = x^{\cdots}$ **(1 mark)**

(c) Simplify

(i) $(x^2)^4 = x^{2\times4} = x^{\cdots}$ **(1 mark)**

(ii) $(x^3)^5 = x^{\cdots}$ **(1 mark)**

**3** (a) Simplify $(2x^3)^4$

$= 2^4 \times (x^3)^4$

Simplify numbers first, then letters.

$= \dots\dots \times x^{\cdots}$ **(2 marks)**

(b) Simplify $(3x^5)^3$

$= \dots\dots\dots\dots$ **(2 marks)**

**4** (a) Simplify $\dfrac{12\,p^4 q^5}{3p^2 q^4}$

$= \dfrac{12}{3} \times \dfrac{p^4}{p^2} \times \dfrac{q^5}{q^4}$

$= \dots\dots\, p^{\cdots}\, q$ **(2 marks)**

$q^1$ is $q$

(b) Simplify $\dfrac{3a^3 b^7}{15ab^6}$

$= \dfrac{\cdots\cdots}{\cdots\cdots}\, a^{\cdots}\, b^{\cdots}$

**(2 marks)**

**5** If $\dfrac{a^{10} \times a^k}{a^5} = a^7$, find $k$.

 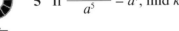

You will need to use problem-solving skills throughout your exam – **be prepared!**

$k = \dots\dots$ **(2 marks)**

**6** Simplify

(a) $2x^2 y^3 \times 3xy^4$

$= 2 \times 3 \times x^2 \times x \times y^3 \times y^4$

$= \dots\dots\, x^{\cdots}\, y^{\cdots}$ **(2 marks)**

(b) $3a^4 b^2 \times 5ab^3$

$= \dots\dots\dots\dots$

**(2 marks)**

# Indices 2

**7** Work out the value of

(a) $25^0$ .......................... $\boxed{x^0 = 1}$ **(1 mark)**

(b) $25^{\frac{1}{2}}$ $= \sqrt{25} =$ .......................... $\boxed{x^{\frac{1}{2}} = \sqrt{x}}$ **(1 mark)**

(c) $25^{-\frac{1}{2}}$ .......................... $\boxed{x^{-\frac{1}{2}} = \frac{1}{x^{\frac{1}{2}}}}$ **(1 mark)**

**8** (a) Simplify $(9x^8)^{\frac{1}{2}}$ $\boxed{\text{Number first, then letters: both to the power } \frac{1}{2}}$  (b) Simplify $(8x^9)^{\frac{1}{3}}$ $\boxed{(x^a)^b = x^{ab}}$

$= 9^{\frac{1}{2}}(x^8)^{\frac{1}{2}} =$ ............ $x^{\cdots}$  **(2 marks)** .............. **(2 marks)**

**9** Work out the value of

(a) $9^{\frac{3}{2}}$ (b) $25^{\frac{3}{2}}$

$= (9^{\frac{1}{2}})^3$ $\boxed{\text{Square root first.}}$ .............. **(2 marks)**

$=$ .............. $^3$

$=$ .............. **(2 marks)**

(c) $8^{-\frac{2}{3}}$ (d) $16^{-\frac{3}{2}}$ $\boxed{\text{One step at a time!}}$

$= (8^{\frac{1}{3}})^{-2}$ $\boxed{x^{\frac{1}{3}} = \sqrt[3]{x}}$ $= (16^{\frac{1}{2}})^{-3}$ $\boxed{\text{Leave your answer as a fraction.}}$

$=$ .............. $^{-2}$ $\boxed{\text{Cube root first.}}$ $=$ .............. 

$= \frac{1}{\ldots^2}$ $\boxed{x^{-2} = \frac{1}{x^2}}$ (e) $\left(\frac{1}{27}\right)^{-\frac{2}{3}}$ **(2 marks)**

$=$ .............. $\boxed{\text{Leave as a fraction.}}$ ..............

**(2 marks)** **(2 marks)**

**10** Write as multiples of prime factors in index form

(a) 256 $\boxed{\text{Use a factor tree first.}}$ (b) 216

 (c) 528

**11** Simplify

(a) $2(3^3)(49^{\frac{1}{2}})(8^{-\frac{1}{3}})$ $\boxed{\text{Look for familiar numbers that you recognise as squares or cubes of other numbers.}}$

(b) $3^4 3^{-2} x^5 x^{-3}$ $\boxed{\text{First rewrite as fractions to get rid of the negative indices, then simplify in the form } 3^{\cdots} x^{\cdots}.}$

(c) $\frac{3x^{\frac{5}{2}}}{7x^{\frac{1}{2}}}$

$= \frac{\ldots}{\ldots} \times \frac{\ldots}{\ldots} x^{\ldots - \ldots}$ $\boxed{\text{The 3 and the 7 are not roots or powers of } x, \text{ so take them out as a factor.}}$

$= -x^{\cdots}$

(d) $16^{\frac{1}{4}}\left(\frac{1}{27}\right)^{-\frac{1}{3}}$

# Calculator skills 1

**1** Write $\frac{11}{32}$ as a decimal.

| 11 | ÷ | 32 | = |

............ **(1 mark)**

> Use **BIDMAS** to remember the correct order of operations:
> **B**rackets
> **I**ndices
> **D**ivision
> **M**ultiplication
> **A**ddition
> **S**ubtraction

**2** Find the value of $\dfrac{\sqrt[3]{140.608}}{(1.2-0.7)^2}$

> Write down the answers to the top and bottom, to show your working.

$= \dfrac{\ldots\ldots}{\ldots\ldots}$

= ............ **(2 marks)**

**3** Find 63% of £157

| 63 | % | × | 157 | = |

£ ............ **(2 marks)**

**4** Toby is going to Thailand on holiday.
The exchange rate is £1 = 43.8 Baht

(a) Toby changes £250 into Baht. How many Baht will he receive?

× 250 ( £1 = 43.8 Baht
         £250 = ............ ) × 250

............................... Baht  **(2 marks)**

**PROBLEM SOLVED!**

(b) When he is in Thailand, Toby wants to buy a necklace for his sister. It cost 525 Baht, how much would that be in pounds? Give your answer to the nearest penny.

> You will need to use problem-solving skills throughout your exam – **be prepared!**

£ ............ **(2 marks)**

**5** (a) Work out $\dfrac{(7.5-1.2)^3}{\sqrt{53.2}}$ giving all the digits on your calculator. ............ **(2 marks)**

**Guided**

(b) Give your answer to 2 decimal places. ............ **(1 mark)**

(c) Give your answer to 3 significant figures. .......... **(1 mark)**

**6** (a) Work out $\dfrac{\sqrt[3]{12.167}}{(3.9+1.2)^2}$ giving all the digits on your calculator. ............ **(2 marks)**

**Guided**

(b) Give your answer to 2 decimal places. ............ **(1 mark)**

(c) Give your answer to 3 significant figures. ............ **(1 mark)**

# Fractions

1  Work out $\frac{3}{5} + \frac{2}{3}$

$= \frac{\ldots}{15} + \frac{\ldots}{15} = \frac{\ldots}{15} = \ldots\frac{\ldots}{15}$

Use equivalent fractions to make a common denominator.

**(1 mark)**

2  Work out $1\frac{3}{4} + \frac{2}{3}$

$= \frac{\ldots}{4} + \frac{2}{3} = \frac{\ldots}{12} + \frac{\ldots}{12} = \frac{\ldots}{12} = 2\frac{\ldots}{12} = \ldots$

Change any mixed fractions to improper fractions.

**(1 mark)**

3  Work out $1\frac{2}{5} \times \frac{5}{6}$

$= \frac{\ldots}{5} \times \frac{5}{6} = \frac{\ldots}{\ldots}$

Multiply top numbers together. Multiply bottom numbers together.

$= \frac{\ldots}{\ldots} = 1\frac{\ldots}{6}$

Simplify.

**(1 mark)**

4  Work out $\frac{2}{3} \div \frac{4}{7}$

$= \frac{2}{3} \times \frac{7}{\ldots}$

Turn 2nd fraction upside down and then multiply.

Multiply tops together, multiply bottoms together.

$= \frac{\ldots}{\ldots} = \frac{\ldots}{\ldots} = 1\frac{\ldots}{\ldots}$

**(1 mark)**

5  (a)  Simplify $\frac{2x}{5} + \frac{x}{10}$

$= \frac{\ldots}{10} + \frac{x}{10}$

Use a common denominator.

$= \frac{\ldots}{10} = \frac{\ldots}{\ldots}$

Simplify.

**(2 marks)**

(b)  Simplify $\frac{3a}{5} \times \frac{2a}{9}$

Multiply tops. Multiply bottoms.

$= \frac{\ldots}{\ldots} = \frac{\ldots}{\ldots}$

Simplify.

**(2 marks)**

(c)  Simplify $\frac{3b^2}{5} \div \frac{3b}{4}$

$= \frac{3b^2}{5} \times \frac{\ldots}{\ldots} = \frac{\ldots}{\ldots} = 9\frac{\ldots b}{\ldots}$

Simplify.

**(2 marks)**

6  Tommy eats $1\frac{1}{3}$ cans of baked beans every day. How many cans does he eat in a week? How many cans does he need to buy?

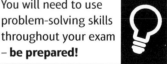
You will need to use problem-solving skills throughout your exam – **be prepared!**

$7 \times 1\frac{1}{3} = \frac{7}{1} \times \frac{\ldots}{3} = \frac{\ldots}{3} = 9\frac{\ldots}{\ldots}$

He needs to buy ............ cans.

**(2 marks)**

7  Vera earns £150 during the weekend. She spends $\frac{2}{5}$ of it on some new jeans and $\frac{1}{3}$ of it on new shoes. How much money does she have left?

You will need to use problem-solving skills throughout your exam – **be prepared!**

............   **(3 marks)**

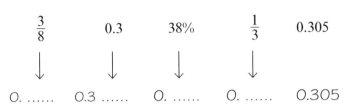

# Decimals

1 Write down these numbers in order of size. Start with the smallest.

$\frac{3}{8}$     0.3     38%     $\frac{1}{3}$     0.305

↓    ↓    ↓    ↓

0. ......   0.3 ......   0. ......   0. ......   0.305

> Change them all to decimals with 3 decimal places.

> Use these to put the original numbers in order of size.

......    ......    ......    ......    ......     **(2 marks)**

2 Given that $62 \times 34 = 2108$

(a) Find the value of $6.2 \times 34$

$= 2108 \div 10 = ......$

> 62 has been divided by 10, so the answer must be divided by 10.

**(1 mark)**

(b) Find the value of $620 \times 3.4$

$= ......$

> 62 has been multiplied by 10 and 34 has been divided by 10.

**(1 mark)**

(c) Find the value of $0.62 \times 3.4$

$= 2108 \div ...... = ......$

> 62 has been divided by 100 and 34 has been divided by 10.

**(1 mark)**

3 Given that $27 \times 82 = 2214$

(a) Find the value of $27 \times 8.2$      ............ **(1 mark)**

(b) Find the value of $2.7 \times 8200$      ............ **(1 mark)**

(c) Find the value of $2214 \div 8.2$      ............ **(1 mark)**

4 Work out $21.6 \times 8.3$

> Work out $216 \times 83$. If there are 2 digits after the decimal points in the question, there will be 2 digits after the decimal point in the answer.

............ **(2 marks)**

5 The cost of a concert ticket is £47.50. How much do 12 tickets cost?

> You will need to use problem-solving skills throughout your exam – **be prepared!**

............ **(2 marks)**

# Estimation

1   Work out an estimate for the value of $89 \times 3.1$

$= 90 \times \ldots\ldots$

$= \ldots\ldots\ldots\ldots\ldots\ldots\ldots$

> Round each number to 1 significant figure.

**(2 marks)**

2   Work out an estimate for the value of $\dfrac{79.42}{7.84 \times 5.43}$

$\approx \dfrac{80}{\ldots\ldots \times 5} = \dfrac{80}{\ldots\ldots} = \ldots\ldots\ldots\ldots\ldots\ldots\ldots\ldots$

> Round each number to 1 significant figure.

**(2 marks)**

3   Work out an estimate for the value of $\dfrac{493.1}{1.91 \times 4.83}$

$\approx \dfrac{\ldots\ldots\ldots\ldots}{\ldots\ldots \times \ldots\ldots} = \ldots\ldots\ldots\ldots\ldots\ldots\ldots\ldots$

**(2 marks)**

4   Work out an estimate for the value of $\dfrac{1.89 \times 27}{0.249}$

$\approx \dfrac{\ldots\ldots \times \ldots\ldots}{0.2} = \dfrac{\ldots\ldots}{0.2} \times \dfrac{\times 10}{\times 10} = \dfrac{\phantom{0}}{2}$

> Multiply the top and bottom by 10 to make the calculation easier.

$\ldots\ldots\ldots\ldots$ **(3 marks)**

5   Work out an estimate for the value of $\dfrac{(5.2 - 1.08)^2}{0.49}$

> You will need to use problem-solving skills throughout your exam – **be prepared!**

**PROBLEM SOLVED!**

$\ldots\ldots\ldots\ldots$ **(3 marks)**

6   Work out an estimate for $\dfrac{213 \times 4.91}{0.19}$

Guided

$\ldots\ldots\ldots\ldots$ **(3 marks)**

7   A football stadium can hold 70 184 spectators. If the price of tickets is £38.50, *estimate* the total amount of money collected in ticket sales.

$70184 \approx \ldots\ldots\ldots$

> Round 70 184 to 1 significant figure.

$£38.50 \approx £\ldots\ldots.00$

> Round £38.50 to 1 significant figure.

So total money $= \ldots\ldots\ldots \times \ldots\ldots\ldots$

$= £\ldots\ldots\ldots$

**(2 marks)**

8   The bill at a restaurant for a meal for 4 people was £88.74. Estimate how much each persion should pay.

Guided

$\ldots\ldots\ldots\ldots$ **(2 marks)**

# Standard form

1 (a) Write 2 150 000 in standard form.

$2\,150\,000 = \ldots\ldots \times 10^{\cdots}$

> What power of 10 have you multiplied by?

> The first number must be between 1 and 10.

**(1 mark)**

(b) Write 0.000312 in standard form.

$0.000\,312 = 3.12 \times 10^{-\cdots}$

> How many times have you divided by 10?

**(1 mark)**

(c) Write 305 000 in standard form.

= ............ **(1 mark)**

(d) Write 0.0072 in standard form.

= ............ **(1 mark)**

2 (a) Write $2.3 \times 10^4$ as an ordinary number.

$= 2\,3\ldots\ldots\ldots$

> Multiply by 10 four times.

**(1 mark)**

(b) Write $6.15 \times 10^{-3}$ as an ordinary number.

$= \ldots\ldots\ldots 6\,1\,5$

> Divide by 10 three times.

**(1 mark)**

(c) Write $1.315 \times 10^6$ as an ordinary number.

= ............ **(1 mark)**

(d) Write $9.012 \times 10^{-4}$ as an ordinary number.

= ............ **(1 mark)**

3 Find the value of $a$ when $a^2 = \dfrac{x+y}{xy}$ and

$x = 2.5 \times 10^5$ and $y = 3 \times 10^6$

> You will need to use problem-solving skills throughout your exam – **be prepared!**

Give your answer in standard form to 2 significant figures.

$x + y = \ldots\ldots\ldots\ldots$ ⎫
$xy = \ldots\ldots\ldots\ldots$ ⎬ so
 

$a^2 = \ldots\ldots\ldots\ldots$
$a = \ldots\ldots\ldots\ldots$

> Use the $\boxed{10^x}$ button on your calculator.

> Show each stage of your working.

**(4 marks)**

4 Find the value of $d$ when $d = \dfrac{xy}{x-y}$ and $x = 4.3 \times 10^7$ and $y = 8.1 \times 10^6$. Give your answer in standard form to 2 significant figures.

> You will need to use problem-solving skills throughout your exam – **be prepared!**

............ **(3 marks)**

# Recurring decimals

 **1** Show that $0.\dot{4}$ can be written as the fraction $\frac{4}{9}$

Let $x = 0.444\,444\,444\ldots$

$10x = 4.444\,444\,444\ldots$

$-\quad x = 0.444\,444\,444\ldots$

$\ldots x = 4$

$x = \ldots$

Multiply by 10.

You are trying to get the numbers after the decimal point to be the same for both $x$ and $10x$. Then, when you subtract one from the other, you will be left with a whole number.

**(2 marks)**

 **2** Change the recurring decimal $0.\dot{2}\dot{5}$ to a fraction.

$x = 0.252\,525\,252\,5\ldots$

$10x = 2.525\,252\,525\,2\ldots$

$100x = 25.252\,525\,252\,5\ldots$

$-\quad x = \quad 0.252\,525\,252\,5\ldots$

$\ldots x = \ldots$

$x = \ldots$

Notice the numbers after the decimal point are not the same so try multiplying by 100.

**(2 marks)**

 **3** Express $0.\dot{3}\dot{0}$ as a fraction in its simplest form.

Remember to simplify your answer.

 ............ **(3 marks)**

 **4** (a) Show $0.\dot{4}\dot{2}$ can be written as $\frac{14}{33}$

 ............ **(2 marks)**

(b) Hence, or otherwise, convert $3.1\dot{4}\dot{2}$ to a mixed number.

Remember to write your answer as a mixed number.

............ **(3 marks)**

 **5** Convert $0.\dot{7}4\dot{1}$ to a fraction in its simplest form.

$x = 0.741\,741\,741\ldots$

$1000x = \ldots\ldots\ldots\ldots\ldots\ldots$

$-\quad x = \quad 0.741\,741\,741\ldots$

$\ldots x = \ldots$

$x = \ldots$

**(3 marks)**

**6** Show $0.2\dot{1}\dot{5}$ can be written as $\frac{71}{330}$

**(3 marks)**

 **7** Prove $0.\dot{9} = 1$

Use the method you have learned above.

 You will need to use problem-solving skills throughout your exam – **be prepared!**

**(2 marks)**

9

# Upper and lower bounds

1　A bag of potatoes weighs 10 kg to the nearest kg.

(a)　What is the minimum possible weight (lower bound weight) of the bag?

$10 - 0.5 = 9.5$ kg ┌─────────────────────────┐ 9.5 rounds up to 10 kg. └─ **(1 mark)**

(b)　What is the maximum possible weight (upper bound weight)
of the bag?

$10 + 0.5 = $ ......... kg　**(1 mark)**

(c)　What is the maximum possible weight of 4 bags?

Upper bound × 4 = ......... × 4 = ......... kg　**(1 mark)**

2　The height of a person measures 176.3 cm, correct to 1 decimal place.

(a)　What is the upper bound of the height?　(b)　What is the lower bound of the height?

$176.3 + 0.05 = $ ........　**(1 mark)**　$176.3 - $ ........ $ = $ ........　**(1 mark)**

3　The length of a rectangle is 152 mm and the width is 10.7 mm, correct to 3 significant figures.

(a)　Find the lower and upper bounds of the rectangle's length and width.

Upper bound of length = $152 + 0.5 = $ ......　Upper bound of width = $10.7 + $ ...... $ = $ ......

Lower bound of length = $152 - $ ...... $ = $ ......　Lower bound of width = $10.7 - 0.05 = $ ......

**(4 marks)**

(b)　Calculate the maximum perimeter of the rectangle. ┌──────────────────────┐ Add together the upper bounds of each of the sides. └──────────────────────┘

............　**(2 marks)**

4　The formula for the speed ($S$) of a car is given by $S = \dfrac{D}{T}$

where $D$ is the distance travelled in km and $T$ is the time taken.

┌─────────────────────────┐ You will need to use problem-solving skills throughout your exam – **be prepared!** └─────────────────────────┘

$D = 142$ km correct to 3 significant figures.
$T = 2.4$ hours correct to 1 decimal place.

By considering bounds, what is the minimum speed in km/h of the car?
Round your final answer to 1 decimal place.

┌──────────────────────────────────────────┐ To calculate the minimum speed, you need to divide the lower bound of the distance by the upper bound of the time. This combination gives you the smallest possible answer. └──────────────────────────────────────────┘

Lower bound of distance = ......

Upper bound of time = ......

$\dfrac{\text{Lower bound of distance}}{\text{Upper bound of time}} = $ ...... $ = $ ...... km/h (1 d.p.)　**(3 marks)**

5　$x = a^2 - b$

┌─────────────────────────┐ You will need to use problem-solving skills throughout your exam – **be prepared!** └─────────────────────────┘

$a = 20.3$ correct to 1 decimal place.
$b = 15$ correct to 2 significant figures.

Calculate the upper bound of $x$. Round your final answer to 3 significant figures.

............　**(4 marks)**

# Accuracy and error

**1** The length of a piece of string is measured to be 12.3 cm, correct to 1 decimal place.

(a) What are the upper and lower bounds of the length?

Upper bound = 12.3 + 0.05 = ...........

Lower bound = ......... − ......... = ...........          **(2 marks)**

(b) Complete this inequality

........... ⩽ length of string < ...........

> This inequality is not 'equal to' as the largest number this can be is actually 12.34999...

**(1 mark)**

**2** The circumference of a circle is 35 mm, rounded to the nearest 5 mm.

(a) Find the upper and lower bounds of the diameter of this circle.

> Circumference = π × diameter

Upper bound of diameter = $\dfrac{..........}{\pi}$ = ...........

Lower bound = $\dfrac{32.5}{\pi}$ = ...........          **(3 marks)**

(b) Complete the inequality

........... ⩽ diameter < ...........          **(1 mark)**

**3** The acceleration of an object is 10 m/s², correct to the nearest integer, and its mass is 50.5 kg, correct to 1 decimal place.

(a) Calculate the upper and lower bounds of the object's force.

> Force = mass × acceleration

Upper bound = ......... × 10.5 = ...........

Lower bound = 50.45 × ......... = ...........          **(2 marks)**

(b) Hence, or otherwise, calculate the force to a suitable degree of accuracy.

> To how many significant figures do you need to round the upper and lower bounds so that you get the same values?

Answer = 500 N (......... s.f.)          **(2 marks)**

**4** A lift can carry 750 kg measured to 2 significant figures. The average weight of a person in the lift is 70 kg measured to the nearest 10 kg.
What is the greatest number of people that can be safely carried in the lift?

...........          **(3 marks)**

**5** A package in the shape of a cube, weighing 948 g, correct to 3 significant figures, is put on a table. It has side length 0.3 m, rounded to the nearest cm.
Pressure (pa) is given by the formula $P = \dfrac{F}{A}$
where $F$ is measured in N and $A$ in m²

> You will need to use problem-solving skills throughout your exam – **be prepared!**

(a) Find the maximum and minimum pressure the package exerts on the table.

**(3 marks)**

(b) Write down the value of $P$ to a suitable degree of accuracy.

**(2 marks)**

# Surds 1

**1** Express the following in the form $a\sqrt{3}$, where $a$ is an integer.

(a) $\sqrt{27} = \sqrt{\underline{9}} \times \sqrt{3} = \underline{3}\sqrt{3}$    | What square number multiplied by 3 gives you 27? |    **(1 mark)**

(b) $\sqrt{75} + \sqrt{300} = \sqrt{\underline{100}} \times \sqrt{3} + \sqrt{\underline{25}} \times \sqrt{3} = \underline{10}\sqrt{3} + \underline{5}\sqrt{3}$   | You can add these surds together. |

    $= \underline{15}\sqrt{3}$                                        **(2 marks)**

| When you multiply $\sqrt{a} \times \sqrt{a}$ you get $a$. |

(c) $\sqrt{3} \times \sqrt{3} \times \sqrt{3}$

    $= \underline{3}\sqrt{3}$                                          **(1 mark)**

(d) $4\sqrt{48} + 2\sqrt{12} = 4 \times \sqrt{\underline{16}} \times \sqrt{3} + 2 \times \sqrt{\underline{4}} \times \sqrt{3} = 16\sqrt{3} + \ldots\sqrt{3} = \ldots\sqrt{3}$    **(2 marks)**

**2** Rationalise the denominators of the following:   | Rationalising means 'getting rid' of the surd in the denominator. |

(a) $\dfrac{7}{\sqrt{6}} \times \dfrac{\sqrt{6}}{\sqrt{6}} = \dfrac{7\sqrt{6}}{6}$    | Multiply the numerator and denominator by $\sqrt{6}$ |    **(1 mark)**

(b) $\dfrac{4}{\sqrt{5}} \times \dfrac{\sqrt{\underline{5}}}{\sqrt{\underline{5}}} = \dfrac{4\sqrt{5}}{\underline{5}}$

(c) $\dfrac{7}{\sqrt{2}} \times \dfrac{\sqrt{2}}{\sqrt{2}} = \dfrac{7\sqrt{2}}{2}$                                **(1 mark)**

(d) $\dfrac{8}{\sqrt{20}} = \dfrac{8}{2\sqrt{5}} = \dfrac{4}{\sqrt{5}} \times \dfrac{\sqrt{5}}{\sqrt{5}} = \dfrac{4\sqrt{5}}{\underline{5}}$    | Sometimes it helps to simplify the denominators first. |    **(2 marks)**

(e) $\dfrac{12}{\sqrt{24}} = \dfrac{12}{\ldots\ldots\ldots\ldots\ldots}$                                **(2 marks)**

**3** Show that $\dfrac{6 + \sqrt{5}}{\sqrt{8}} = \dfrac{6\sqrt{2} + \sqrt{10}}{4}$    | $\sqrt{a} \times \sqrt{b} = \sqrt{ab}$ |

$\dfrac{6 + \sqrt{5}}{\sqrt{8}} \times \dfrac{\ldots\ldots}{\ldots\ldots} = \dfrac{\ldots + \sqrt{40}}{8} = \dfrac{\ldots\sqrt{2} + \ldots\sqrt{10}}{8} = \dfrac{\ldots\sqrt{2} + \ldots\sqrt{10}}{4}$    **(2 marks)**

**4** Calculate the length of the diagonal $AC$ in this rectangle.
Write your answer in the form $a\sqrt{b}$ where $a$ and $b$ are integers.

| You will need to use problem-solving skills throughout your exam – **be prepared!** |

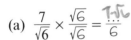

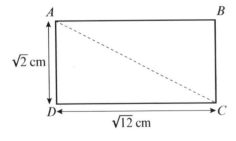

| Pythagoras' theorem |

                                                   $\ldots\ldots\ldots\ldots$   **(3 marks)**

**5** Calculate the area of a triangle with perpendicular height $\sqrt{10}$ m and base $\dfrac{1}{\sqrt{2}}$ m.
Write your answer in the form $\dfrac{\sqrt{a}}{b}$, where $a$ and $b$ are integers.

| You will need to use problem-solving skills throughout your exam – **be prepared!** |

                                                   $\ldots\ldots\ldots\ldots$   **(3 marks)**

**6** Rationalise the denominator of $\dfrac{5 + \sqrt{7}}{\sqrt{7} + 1}$

$\dfrac{5 + \sqrt{7}}{\sqrt{7} + 1} \times \dfrac{\sqrt{7} - 1}{\sqrt{7} - 1} = \ldots\ldots\ldots\ldots$                  **(3 marks)**

# Counting strategies

**1** Tom has 3 numbered cards.

  (a) List the possible 3 digit numbers he can make.

    (123), (132), (2 ......), (2 ......). (3 ......), (......)        **(1 mark)**

  (b) What is the probability Tom's 3 digit number is even?

$$\frac{...}{6} = \frac{......}{......}$$        **(1 mark)**

**2** In a restaurant, Claire has the choice of 4 starters, 3 mains and 5 desserts. How many possible outcomes are there if Claire has to pick one starter, main and dessert?

> If you have $x$ ways for choice 1, $y$ ways for choice 2, and $z$ ways for choice 3 then there are $xyz$ ways for all three choices.

    $4 \times$ ............ $\times$ ............ $=$ ............        **(2 marks)**

**3** Rohan has three coloured counters. He needs to pick two counters. How many possible combinations are there?

> How many ways are there of picking the 1st counter? Now a counter has been picked, how many ways are there of picking the 2nd counter?

    $3 \times$ ............ $=$ ............        **(2 marks)**

**4** (a) A safe has numbers 0–5. The safe needs three digits to unlock it.

    Owen says there are $6 \times 5 \times 4$ ways of picking 3 digits.
    Nim says there are $6 \times 6 \times 6$ ways of picking 3 digits.
    Who is correct and why?

> You will need to use problem-solving skills throughout your exam – **be prepared!**

    ................................................................................................................

    ................................................................................................................    **(2 marks)**

  (b) Another safe has numbers 0–5 and letters A–N. This safe needs one number and two letters to unlock, of which each number and letter can only be used once. How many possible outcomes are there?

> How many letters are left to choose from?

Number    Letter        Letter

       6    $\times$    14    $\times$     ............ $=$ ............

> You will need to use problem-solving skills throughout your exam – **be prepared!**

                                           **(2 marks)**

**5** There are 12 players left to be picked from for the starting line-up of a football match. The coach needs to pick 4 players. How many different ways can he do this?

                                                   ............ **(2 marks)**

# Problem-solving practice 1

**1** Find $n$ when $4^{\frac{1}{2}} \times 8^{-\frac{2}{3}} = 2^n$

$(2^{\cdots})^{\frac{1}{2}} \times (2^{\cdots})^{-\frac{2}{3}} = 2^n$

$2^{\cdots} \times 2^{\cdots} = 2^n$

$2^{\cdots} = 2^n$

> Write 4 and 8 as powers of 2.

> $(2^a)^b = 2^{ab}$

> $2^a \times 2^b = 2^{a+b}$

$n = \ldots\ldots\ldots\ldots$ **(4 marks)**

**2** 1 astronomical unit, the distance between the Sun and Earth, is $1.5 \times 10^8$ km. The distance between Earth and Neptune is 29 astronomical units.

(a) What is the distance between Earth and Neptune in km? Give your answer in standard form.

$29 \times \ldots\ldots\ldots\ldots = \ldots\ldots\ldots\ldots$ km **(2 marks)**

(b) The distance between Mars and Venus is $8 \times 10^{-1}$ astronomical units. What is this distance in km, in standard form?

$\ldots\ldots\ldots\ldots \times \ldots\ldots\ldots\ldots = \ldots\ldots\ldots\ldots$ km **(2 marks)**

**3** Two toy cars are started from the same point on a circular track at different speeds. Car A and car B take 24 and 40 seconds, respectively, to complete the track. After how long will the cars next pass the start point at the same time?

> Find the HCF of 24 and 40.

$\ldots\ldots\ldots\ldots$ **(2 marks)**

**4** There are 500 pupils in a school. They travel there by car, bicycle or by walking. $\frac{1}{4}$ of the children cycle to school. $\frac{2}{5}$ of those who cycle are girls. The number of girls coming to school by car is twice the number who cycle. 175 children walk, of those 60 are boys. How many boys come to school by car?

It may help to draw a 2-way table

$\frac{1}{4}$ of 500 = 125

$\frac{2}{5}$ of 125 = ........

Each part of the question helps you to fill in the table

|        | Bicycle | Car     | Walk    | Total   |
|--------|---------|---------|---------|---------|
| Girls  | ........ | ........ | ........ | ........ |
| Boys   | ........ | ........ | ........ | ........ |
| Total  | 125     | ........ | ........ | 500     |

$\ldots\ldots\ldots\ldots$ **(4 marks)**

# Problem-solving practice 2

**5** A lawn, in the shape of a parallelogram, has the dimensions shown.

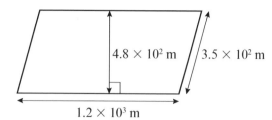

$4.8 \times 10^2$ m   $3.5 \times 10^2$ m

$1.2 \times 10^3$ m

(a) What is the perimeter of the lawn? Give your answer in standard form.

............   **(2 marks)**

(b) What is the area of the lawn? Give your answer in standard form.

............   **(2 marks)**

**6** The resistance (ohms), of an electrical component is measured by the formula

$$R = \frac{V}{I}$$

$V = 350$ volts, correct to 2 significant figures.

$I = 15$ amps, correct to the nearest amp.

(a) What are the minimum and maximum possible values for the resistance?

............   **(3 marks)**

(b) Calculate the resistance to a suitable degree of accuracy. Explain your choice.

............   **(2 marks)**

**7** What are the next two terms of the following geometric sequences?

(a) $3\sqrt{5}$, 15, $15\sqrt{5}$, 75, ........., .........

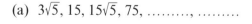

**(2 marks)**

(b) $2\sqrt{3}$, 12, $24\sqrt{3}$, 144, ........., .........

**(2 marks)**

# Algebraic expressions

**1** (a) Simplify $x + x + x + x$

=   ...**4**.$x$

> Count how many $x$s there are.    **(1 mark)**

(b) Simplify $x + x + y + y + y$

=   ..**2**..$x$ + ..**3**..$y$

> Count the $x$s and $y$s separately.    **(1 mark)**

**2** (a) Simplify $2x + y + 3x + 2y$

=   ..**5**..$x$ + ..**3**..$y$

> Ring round each term including its + or − sign and collect 'like' terms.    **(1 mark)**

(b) Simplify $3a − b − a − 3b$

=   ...**2**.$a$ − ..**4**..$b$

> Be careful with minus signs − $b − 3b = ?$    **(1 mark)**

(c) Simplify $3p^2 + 2p + 4p^2 − 5p$

=   ...**7**.$p^2$ + ......$p$

> Remember that $p^2$ and $p$ are not 'like' terms.    **(2 marks)**

**3** (a) Simplify $2x \times 3x$

= $\underbrace{2 \times 3}$ × $\underbrace{x \times x}$

=   ...**6**$x^2$........

> Multiply the numbers first, then the letters    **(1 mark)**

(b) Simplify $3xy^2 \times 5x^2y$

= $\underbrace{3 \times 5}$   ×   $\underbrace{x \times x^2}$   ×   $\underbrace{y^2 \times y}$

= ........................................

> Remember that $x$ is $x^1$.    **(2 marks)**

(c) Simplify $7a^2b^3c \times 5ab^4c^2$

= .................

    **(2 marks)**

**4** (a) Simplify $\dfrac{4x^3}{2x}$

> Divide top and bottom by 2.

= $\dfrac{4 \times \cancel{x} \times x \times x \times x}{2 \times x}$

> Divide top and bottom by common terms.

= 2......

    **(2 marks)**

(b) Simplify $\dfrac{12x^4y^2}{15x^3y^5}$

= $\dfrac{12 \times x \times x \times x \times x \times y \times y}{15 \times x \times x \times x \times y \times y \times y \times y \times y}$

> Divide top and bottom by 3.

= $\dfrac{4........}{5........}$

    **(2 marks)**

(c) Simplify $\dfrac{25\,x^2y^3z^4}{10\,x^4y^2z^4}$

= .................

> You will need to use problem-solving skills throughout your exam – **be prepared!**    **(2 marks)**

**PROBLEM SOLVED!**

# Expanding brackets

**1** (a) Expand $5(2x + 3)$

$= 10x + 15$

> Multiply the term in front by each term in the brackets.

**(1 mark)**

(b) Expand $3x(2x - 5)$

$= 6x^2 - 15x$     **(1 mark)**

(c) Expand $2a^2(3a - 7)$

$= 6a^3 - 14a^2$     **(1 mark)**

**2** (a) Expand and simplify

$2(2x + 3) + 3(5x - 1)$

$= 4x + 6 + 15x - 3$

$= 19x + 3$

> Multiply out each of the brackets, then collect the like terms.

**(2 marks)**

(b) Expand and simplify

$4(3x - 2) - 5(2x - 1)$

> Remember
> $-5 \times -1 = +5$

$= 12x - 8 - 10x + 5$

> Multiply out each bracket.

$= 2x - 3$

> Collect like terms.  **(2 marks)**

(c) Expand and simplify

$3(2 - 5b) + 4(2b + 3)$

$6 - 15b + 8b + 12$

$= 23b - 12$     **(2 marks)**

$18 - 7b$

**3** (a) Expand and simplify

$\overset{F}{(x} + \overset{L}{5)} \; (x + 2)$

$= x^2 + 2x + 5x + 10$

$= x^2 + 7x + 10$

> Multiply the:
> First     terms
> Outside   terms
> Inside    terms
> Last      terms
>
> FOIL method

**(2 marks)**

(b) Expand and simplify $(x - 3)(x + 4)$

$= x^2 + 4x - 3x - 12$

$= x^2 + 1x - 12$

**(2 marks)**

(c) Expand and simplify $(2x - 5)(x - 3)$

$= 2x^2 - 6x - 5x + 15$

> Remember $- \times -$ is a $+$.

> Collect like terms.

$= 2x^2 - 11x + 15$

**(2 marks)**

(d) Expand and simplify $(3x - 1)(2x + 5)$

$= 6x^2 + 13x - 5$

**(2 marks)**

**4** You may prefer the grid method to expand two brackets, e.g. Expand $(x + 5)(2x - 3)$

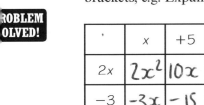

> You will need to use problem-solving skills throughout your exam – **be prepared!**

|     | $x$    | $+5$  |
|-----|--------|-------|
| $2x$ | $2x^2$ | $10x$ |
| $-3$ | $-3x$  | $-15$ |

> Multiply terms together to fill in each box, then add the terms together.

$= 2x^2 + 10x - 3x - 15$

$= x^2 + 7x - 15$

**(2 marks)**

**PROBLEM SOLVED!**

# Factorising

1  (a)  Factorise $10x + 15$

$= 5(\ldots x + \ldots)$

> What is common to both terms? Bring this out, in front of the brackets.
>
> Then ask, what do I need to multiply this by to get 10x and then 15?

**(1 mark)**

(b)  Factorise $6x - 18$

$= 6(\ldots x - \ldots)$

**(1 mark)**

(c)  Factorise $x^2 - 7x$

$= x(\ldots - \ldots)$

> Sometimes it is a letter that is common to both.

**(1 mark)**

(d)  Factorise $12x^2 + 15x$

$= 3x(\ldots x + \ldots)$

> Sometimes it is a letter and a number!

**(1 mark)**

(e)  Factorise $9xy - 12x^2$

$= \ldots\ldots (\ldots\ldots\ldots\ldots)$

**(1 mark)**

(f)  Factorise $25y^3 + 20y^2$

$= \ldots\ldots\ldots\ldots\ldots\ldots$

**(1 mark)**

2  (a)  Factorise $x^2 + 7x + 12$

$= (x + \ldots)(x + \ldots)$

> A quadratic factorises into 2 brackets.

> These numbers need to multiply together to make 12, but add together to make 7.

**(2 marks)**

(b)  Factorise $x^2 - 6x + 8$

$= (x - \ldots)(x - \ldots)$

> The two numbers need to multiply together to get +8, but add together to get −6. (Remember − × − is a + !)

**(2 marks)**

(c)  Factorise $x^2 - 3x - 10$

$= (x + \ldots)(x - \ldots)$

> Remember to check your answer by multiplying out the brackets to get back to the question.

**(2 marks)**

(d)  Factorise $x^2 + 2x - 15$

$= (\ldots\ldots\ldots)(\ldots\ldots\ldots)$

**(2 marks)**

3  (a)  Factorise $2x^2 + 7x + 3$

$= (2x + \ldots)(x + \ldots)$

> The numbers must multiply together to get +3, but also the inside terms added to the outside terms must make +7x.

**(2 marks)**

(b)  Factorise $3x^2 - 2x - 5$

$= (3x \ldots)(x \ldots)$

> The 2 numbers multiply together to get −5; inside and outside terms add to get −2x.

**(2 marks)**

(c)  Factorise $5x^2 - 14x - 3$

$= (\ldots\ldots\ldots)(\ldots\ldots\ldots)$

**(2 marks)**

4  (a)  Factorise $x^2 - y^2$

$(x + \ldots\ldots)(x - \ldots\ldots)$

> A special case called 'the difference of two squares'.

**(2 marks)**

(b)  Factorise $4x^2 - 9y^2$

$(2x \ldots\ldots)(2x \ldots\ldots)$

> The 2 brackets will have the same terms but different signs so that the inside and outside terms cancel out.

**(2 marks)**

(c)  Factorise $25a^2 - 81$

$= (\ldots\ldots)(\ldots\ldots)$

**(2 marks)**

# Linear equations 1

**1** (a) Solve $2x - 5 = 3$

$2x = \ldots$

$x = \ldots$

> Add 5 to both sides.

> Divide both sides by 2.

> Check your answer is correct by substituting it back into the question!

**(2 marks)**

(b) Solve $1 + 3x = 7$

$3x = \ldots$

$x = \ldots$

> Subtract 1 from both sides.

> Divide both sides by 3.

**(2 marks)**

(c) Solve $3(2x - 3) = 4$

> Multiply out the brackets first.

$\ldots x - \ldots = 6$

$\ldots x = \ldots$

$x = \ldots$        **(2 marks)**

(d) Solve $15 = 3(2x + 3)$

$x = \ldots\ldots\ldots$        **(2 marks)**

**2** (a) Solve $3x + 2 = x + 11$

$\ldots x + 2 = 11$

$\ldots x = \ldots$

$x = \ldots$

> Subtract $x$ from both sides.

> Subtract 2 from both sides.

> Now divide by the number of $x$s.

**(2 marks)**

(b) Solve $2x - 1 = 5x - 16$

$-1 = \ldots x - 16$

> Subtract 2x from both sides.

$\ldots = \ldots x$

> Add 16 to both sides.

$x = \ldots$        **(2 marks)**

(c) Solve $6x - 5 = 4x - 1$

$x = \ldots$        **(2 marks)**

**3** (a) Solve $2 - 3x = -1$

$2 = -1 + 3x$

> Add 3x to both sides.

$\ldots = 3x$

> Add 1 to both sides.

$x = \ldots$

> Now divide by 3.

**(2 marks)**

(b) Solve $5 - 2x = 2x - 3$

$5 = \ldots x - 3$

> Add 2x to both sides.

$\ldots = \ldots x$

> Add 3 to both sides.

$x = \ldots$

> Now divide by the number of $x$s.

**(2 marks)**

(c) Solve $4 - 3x = 10 - 5x$

$4 + \ldots x = 10$

$\ldots x = \ldots$

$x = \ldots$

> Add 5x to both sides.

> Subtract 4 from both sides.

> Divide by the number of $x$s.        **(2 marks)**

(d) Solve $6 - 2x = x - 3$

> You will need to use problem-solving skills throughout your exam – **be prepared!**

**PROBLEM SOLVED!**

$x = \ldots$        **(2 marks)**

# Linear equations 2

**4** (a) Solve $\frac{x}{5} = 4$

  $x = \ldots$ | Multiply both sides by 5. | **(1 mark)**

(b) Solve $\frac{a}{3} = 7$

  $a = \ldots$ **(1 mark)**

**5** (a) Solve $5 + \frac{x}{2} = 8$ | Subtract 5 from both sides. |

  $\frac{x}{2} = \ldots$ | Multiply both sides by 2. |

  $x = \ldots$ **(2 marks)**

(b) Solve $2 = \frac{a}{3} - 4$

  $a = \ldots$ **(2 marks)**

**6** (a) Solve $\frac{x-2}{3} = 1$

  $x - 2 = \ldots$

  $x = \ldots$

  | Multiply both sides by 3. |
  | Add 2 to both sides. | **(2 marks)**

(b) Solve $7 = \frac{x-1}{2} + 3$

  $\ldots = \frac{x-1}{2}$

  $\ldots = x - 1$

  $\ldots = x$

  | Subtract 3 from both sides. |
  | Multiply both sides by 2. |
  | Add 1 to both sides. | **(2 marks)**

(c) Solve $4 + \frac{x+3}{2} = -1$

  $x = \ldots$ **(2 marks)**

**7** (a) The perimeter of the rectangle is 18 cm, find the value of $x$.

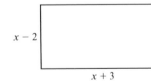

(Diagram not accurately drawn)

$2(x - 2) + 2(x + 3) = 18$

$\ldots x - \ldots + \ldots x + \ldots = 18$

$\ldots x + \ldots = 18$

$\ldots x = \ldots$

$x = \ldots$ cm

| Expand brackets. |
| Collect like terms. |
| Solve the equation. |

**PROBLEM SOLVED!**

You will need to use problem-solving skills throughout your exam – **be prepared!**

**(3 marks)**

**PROBLEM SOLVED!**

(b) Find the size of the smallest angle in the triangle below.

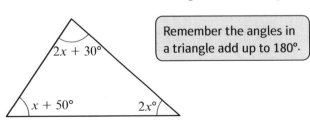

| Remember the angles in a triangle add up to 180°. |

You will need to use problem-solving skills throughout your exam – **be prepared!**

$\ldots\ldots\ldots\ldots$ ° **(3 marks)**

# Formulae

1  (a)  Using the formula $a = 3b - c$, find $a$ when $b = 2$ and $c = 1$.

$a = 3 \times \ldots - \ldots$

$a = \ldots$                                                                        **(2 marks)**

(b)  Find the value of $u$ in the formula $u = v^2 - wz$
when $v = -2$, $w = 5$ and $z = -1$.

$u = (-2)^2 - 5 \times (-1)$

> Replace the letters in the formula with the given numbers.

$u = \ldots + \ldots$

> Remember $- \times - = +$ !

$u = \ldots$                                                                        **(2 marks)**

(c)  $d = \dfrac{e^2 - f}{g}$     Find the value of $d$ when $e = -3$, $f = -3$ and $g = 2$.

$d = \ldots\ldots\ldots\ldots\ldots$                                               **(2 marks)**

2  (a)  (i)  Pens cost 30p each, what is the cost of $x$ pens?          $\ldots x$ pence          **(1 mark)**

(ii)  Pencils cost 10p each, what is the cost of $y$ pencils?          $\ldots y$ pence          **(1 mark)**

(iii)  What is the total cost, £$C$, of $x$ pens and $y$ pencils?       $C = \dfrac{\ldots x + \ldots y}{100}$          **(2 marks)**

(iv)  What is the total cost, in pounds, of 6 pens and 5 pencils?

£$\ldots$          **(2 marks)**

(b)  Apples cost 35p each and bananas cost 45p each. Write a formula for the
total cost, £$C$, of $x$ apples and $y$ bananas.

$C = \ldots\ldots\ldots\ldots\ldots$                                               **(2 marks)**

3  Jon looked up, on the internet, the time it will take to cook a turkey. The instructions given
were: 'If the turkey is over 4 kg, calculate 20 minutes per kilogram plus an extra 90 minutes.'

(a)  Write a formula for the total time needed, $T$,
in minutes, to cook a turkey that weighs $W$ kg.

> You will need to use problem-solving skills throughout your exam – **be prepared!**
>

$T = \ldots W + \ldots$          **(1 mark)**

(b)  Find the time needed to cook a 6 kg turkey. Give your answer in hours and minutes.

$T = \ldots \times 6 + \ldots$

$= \ldots$ minutes

> Remember 60 minutes = 1 hour.

$= \ldots$ hours $\ldots$ minutes          **(2 marks)**

4  The tariff used to calculate an electricity bill at the end of the
year is given by:

> You will need to use problem-solving skills throughout your exam – **be prepared!**
>

'The total cost is 12p per kilowatt hour plus a standing charge
of £76.60'

(a)  Write a formula for annual cost, £$C$, for using $K$ kWh
of electricity.

> 12p = £0.12

$\ldots\ldots\ldots\ldots$          **(2 marks)**

(b)  Find the cost of using 3600 kWh of electricity in a year.

£ $\ldots\ldots\ldots\ldots$          **(1 mark)**

# Arithmetic sequences

1   Here are the first four terms of a sequence

*zero term*

    −2.     2     6     10     14     .18.     22.

    −4    +.4.   +.4.   +.4.   +.4.   +.4

(a)   Write down the next two terms in the sequence.      **(1 mark)**

(b)   Find an expression for the $n$th term of the sequence.      **(1 mark)**

    $n$th term = ...... $n$ − ......

$n$th term = difference between terms × $n$ + zero term    **(2 marks)**

2   Find an expression for the $n$th term of the sequence

        +1    4     7    10    ......

    $n$th term = ............ $n$ − ............      **(2 marks)**

3   (a)   Find an expression for the $n$th term of the sequence

> Guided

          10     8     6     4    ......

    $n$th term = ..............      **(2 marks)**

(b)   Find the 100th term of this sequence.

                                  ..............    **(1 mark)**

4   (a)   Find an expression for the $n$th term of the sequence

> Guided

        7     11     15     19    ......

    $n$th term = ..............      **(2 marks)**

(b)   Is it possible that 82 is a term in this sequence? Explain your answer.

What type of numbers are in the sequence?

**PROBLEM SOLVED!**

You will need to use problem-solving skills throughout your exam – **be prepared!**    **(2 marks)**

5   The $n$th term of a sequence is $3n - 2$.

**PROBLEM SOLVED!**

(a)   Find the first four terms of the sequence.

You will need to use problem-solving skills throughout your exam – **be prepared!**

    1st term = $3 \times 1 - 2$ = ......

    2nd term = $3 \times 2 - 2$ = ......

    3rd term = $3 \times$ ...... $- 2$ = ......

    4th term = ...... $\times$ ...... $-$ ...... = ......      **(2 marks)**

(b)   Find the 60th term in this sequence.

                                    ..............    **(1 mark)**

# Solving sequence problems

**1** Draw lines to match a sequence with its name.

| cube | | 1 | 3 | 6 | 10 | 15 |
| square | | 1 | 1 | 2 | 3 | 5 |
| triangular | | 1 | 4 | 9 | 16 | 25 |
| fibonacci | | 1 | 8 | 27 | 64 | 125 |

**(2 marks)**

**2** Are the following sequences geometric progressions?
You must give reasons for your answers.

(a) 2   6   18   36

> Are you multiplying by the same number each time?

× ... × ... × ...

......, because ............................................................................. **(2 marks)**

(b) 4   2   1   $\frac{1}{2}$

× ... × ... × ...

......, because ............................................................................. **(2 marks)**

**3** The first seven terms of a Fibonacci sequence are

$$1 \quad 1 \quad 2 \quad 3 \quad 5 \quad 8 \quad 13$$

> In a Fibonacci sequence, the next term is found by adding up the two terms before it.

(a) Find the 10th term in this sequence. ............ **(1 mark)**

(b) The first two terms of another Fibonacci sequence are

$x \quad y$

Show that the 5th term of this sequence is $2x + 3y$.

1st term $= x$
2nd term $= y$
3rd term $= x + y$
4th term $= y + x + y = ... + ...$
5th term $= ............ + ............$
      $= ...x + ...y$

> You will need to use problem-solving skills throughout your exam – **be prepared!**

> 4th term = 2nd term + 3rd term

> 5th term = 3rd term + 4th term

**(3 marks)**

(c) If the 3rd term is 4 and the 5th term is 11, find $x$ and $y$.

$x + y = 4$

$...x + ...y = 11$

> You will need to use problem-solving skills throughout your exam – **be prepared!**

> Write 2 equations and solve them simultaneously.

$x = ..., y = ...$    **(3 marks)**

# Quadratic sequences

**1**  Find an expression for the $n$th term of the sequence

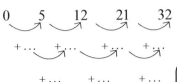

0    5    12    21    32

$+...$    $+...$    $+...$    $+...$

$+...$    $+...$    $+...$

> Find the differences.

> Find the 2nd row of differences.

> What are the differences of the differences?

> If the 2nd row of differences are the same, the sequence is quadratic. If they are all +2, there is an $n^2$ in the formula.

| Sequence | 0 | 5 | 12 | 21 | 32 |
|----------|-----|-----|-----|-----|-----|
| $n^2$    | 1 | 4 | 9 | 16 | 25 |
| residue  | −1 | 1 | 3 | ... | ... |

> Subtract $n^2$ from the sequence.

$n$th term of the residue .........$n - $.........

Therefore $T = n^2 + $.........$n - $.........

**(4 marks)**

**2**  Find an expression for the $n$th term of the sequence

5        7        11        17        25

1st row of diff.:    ......    ......    ......    ......

2nd row of diff.:    ......    ......    ......

**PROBLEM SOLVED!**

Sequence

$n^2$

........................................................

residue

> You will need to use problem-solving skills throughout your exam – **be prepared!**

$n$th term for residue =

So complete formula is $T = $...........

**(4 marks)**

**3**  Find an expression for the $n$th term of the sequence

9        12        19        30        45

......    ......    ......    ......

......    ......    ......

**Guided** ~~✗~~

**PROBLEM SOLVED!**

> You will need to use problem-solving skills throughout your exam – **be prepared!**

> If the 2nd row of differences is  2  there will be  $n^2$  in the sequence.
>
> If the 2nd row of differences is  4  there will be  $2n^2$  in the sequence.
>
> If the 2nd row of differences is  $a$  there will be  $\frac{a}{2}n^2$  in the sequence.

...........    **(4 marks)**

# Straight-line graphs 1

**1** (a) Find the gradient of this line.

$$\text{Gradient} = \frac{\text{distance up}}{\text{distance across}} = \frac{......}{......}$$

$$= \text{............} \quad \textbf{(2 marks)}$$

(b) Find the $y$-intercept of this line.

> The $y$-intercept is where the line crosses the $y$-axis.

............ **(1 mark)**

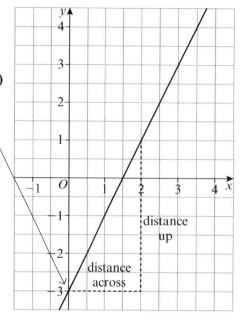

(c) Find the equation of this line.

> The equation of a straight-line graph is $y = mx + c$ where $m$ is the gradient and $c$ is the $y$-intercept.

$$y = \underset{\underset{\text{gradient}}{\uparrow}}{......} \; x - \underset{\underset{\text{y-intercept}}{\uparrow}}{......}$$

**(2 marks)**

**2** (a) Find the gradient of this line.

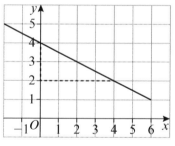

Gradient =

> If the line slopes down: ＼ then it has a negative gradient. ＼

............ **(2 marks)**

(b) Find the $y$-intercept of this line.

............ **(1 mark)**

(c) Find the equation of this line.

$$y = ...... \, x \, ......$$

............ **(2 marks)**

# Straight-line graphs 2

**3** (a) Complete the table of values for the graph of $2x + y = 5$.

| $x$ | $-1$ | 0 | 1 | 2 | 3 | 4 |
|-----|------|---|---|---|---|---|
| $y$ | 7 | | | | $-1$ | |

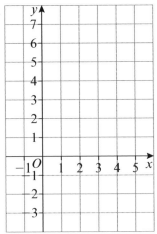

> Put the values of $x$ into the function to find each value of $y$.

$x = 0$: $2 \times 0$ $+ y = 5$     $y = \ldots\ldots$

$x = 1$: $2 \times 1$ $+ y = 5$     $y = \ldots\ldots$

$x = 2$

**(2 marks)**

(b) On the grid, draw the graph of $2x + y = 5$ for values of $x$ from $-1$ to 3.

> Plot the points from the table and draw a straight line through them.

**(2 marks)**

**4** (a) Find the gradient of the line with equation $3y - 2x = 6$.

$(+2x)$   $3y = \ldots\ldots x + 6$

> Rearrange the equation to make $y$ the subject.

$(-3)$   $y = \ldots\ldots x + \ldots\ldots$

> The gradient is the value in front of $x$.

Gradient $= \ldots\ldots$

**(2 marks)**

(b) Find an equation of the line with gradient $-2$ that passes through the point $(1, 1)$.

**PROBLEM SOLVED!**

> You will need to use problem-solving skills throughout your exam – **be prepared!**

> The equation is $y = mx + c$, where $m$ is the gradient.

> To find $c$, put in the values $x = 1$ and $y = 1$.

> Now find $c$.

$1 = \ldots\ldots \times 1 + c$

$c = \ldots\ldots$

So $y = \ldots\ldots x + \ldots\ldots$

**(2 marks)**

**5** (a) The equation of a line $L$ is $2y - x = 4$.
Find the gradient of $L$.

$y = \ldots\ldots\ldots\ldots$

> Rearrange to make $y$ the subject, and look for the value in front of $x$.

Gradient is $\ldots\ldots$

**(2 marks)**

(b) Find the equation of the line which is parallel to $L$ and passes through the point $(4, 1)$.

**PROBLEM SOLVED!**

$y = \ldots\ldots x + c$

> Parallel lines have the same gradient.

> You will need to use problem-solving skills throughout your exam – **be prepared!**

$c = \ldots\ldots$

> To find $c$, put in $x = 4$, $y = 1$.

So $y = \ldots\ldots x - \ldots\ldots$

**(2 marks)**

# Parallel and perpendicular

**1** Here are the equations of 4 straight lines.

A: $y = \frac{1}{3}x - 1$     B: $y = -3x + 5$     C: $y = 3x - 5$     D: $y = -\frac{1}{3}x + 2$

(a) Write down the letter of the line that is parallel to

$y = \frac{1}{3}x + 2$.          D

Parallel lines have the same gradient.

$A \quad y = \frac{1}{3}x - 5$          **(1 mark)**

(b) Write down the letter of the line that is perpendicular to $y = 3x + 1$.

D          If a line has gradient $m$, a perpendicular line will have a gradient $-\frac{1}{m}$.

$B \quad y = -5x + 1$          **(1 mark)**

**2** A straight line, $L$, passes through the point $(2, 5)$ and is perpendicular to the line with equation $y = -2x + 1$. Find the equation of the line $L$.

The gradient of the line $y = -2x + 1$ is ...$-2$...

You will need to use problem-solving skills throughout your exam – **be prepared!**

The gradient of a line perpendicular to this line is $-\frac{1}{2}$

So the equation of $L$ is $y = -\frac{1}{2}x + c$

To find $c$, substitute the values $x = 2$ and $y = 5$ into $L$:

$5 = -\frac{1}{2} \times 2 + c$          Rearrange to find $c$.

$c = ......$

So the equation of $L$ is $y = ...... x + ......$          **(3 marks)**

**3** $A$ has coordinates $\underset{\underset{x_1 \; y_1}{\uparrow \; \uparrow}}{(3, 3)}$ and $B$ has coordinates $\underset{\underset{x_2 \; y_2}{\uparrow \; \uparrow}}{(5, 7)}$.

(a) Find the midpoint of $AB$.

Midpoint $= \left( \dfrac{x_1 + x_2}{2}, \dfrac{y_1 + y_2}{2} \right)$

$\dfrac{... + ...}{2}, \dfrac{... + ...}{2} = (......, ......)$          **(2 marks)**

(b) Find the gradient of the line $AB$.

Gradient $= \dfrac{... - ...}{... - ...}$          Gradient $= \dfrac{y_2 - y_1}{x_2 - x_1}$

$= \dfrac{...}{...} = ...$          **(2 marks)**

(c) Find the equation of the line that is perpendicular to $AB$ and passes through the midpoint of $AB$.

You will need to use problem-solving skills throughout your exam – **be prepared!**

Gradient of perpendicular $= -\dfrac{1}{......}$

So line has equation $y = ... x + c$

To find $c$, substitute the $x$ and $y$ values of the midpoint and rearrange.

So line has equation $y = ... x + ...$          **(3 marks)**

# Quadratic graphs

**1** (a) Complete the table for $y = x^2 - 3x + 1$.

| $x$ | $-1$ | 0 | 1 | 2 | 3 | 4 |
|-----|------|---|----|---|---|---|
| $y$ |      |   | $-1$ |   |   | 5 |

**(2 marks)**

$x = -1$:  $y = (-1)^2 - 3 \times (-1) + 1 =$ .........

$x = 3$:  $y = 3^2 - 3 \times 3 + 1 =$ .........

> Substitute the $x$ values into the function.

(b) On the grid, draw the graph of $y = x^2 - 3x + 1$.

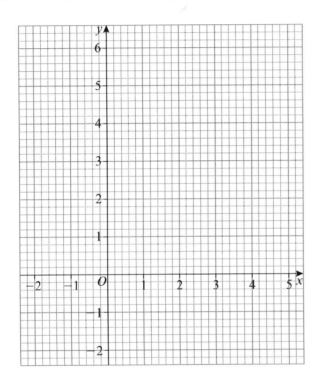

> Plot the points and join with a smooth curve.

**(2 marks)**

(c) Use the graph to find a minimum value of $y$.

> Read off the value of $y$ for the bottom tip of the curve.

$y =$ ........... **(1 mark)**

(d) Use the graph to solve $x^2 - 3x + 1 = 0$.

$x =$ ........... or ........... **(2 marks)**

(e) Use the graph to solve $x^2 - 3x + 1 = 2$.

$x =$ ........... or ........... **(2 marks)**

# Cubic and reciprocal graphs

**1** (a) Complete the table for $y = x^3 - 4x^2 + 5$.

| $x$ | $-1$ | 0 | 1 | 2 | 3 | 4 |
|---|---|---|---|---|---|---|
| $y$ | | | 2 | | $-4$ | |

when $x = -1$: $y = (-1)^3 - 4 \times (-1)^2 + 5 = $ ......

when $x = 4$: $y = 4^3 - 4 \times 4^2 + 5 = $ ......

> Substitute the *x* values into the function to find *y*.

**(2 marks)**

(b) On the grid, draw the graph of $y = x^3 - 4x^2 + 5$.

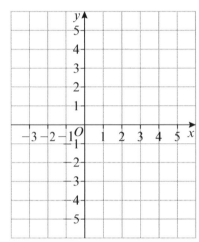

> Plot the points and draw a smooth curve through them.

**(2 marks)**

**2** (a) Complete the table for $y = \frac{2}{x}$.

| $x$ | 0.5 | 1 | 2 | 4 | 5 |
|---|---|---|---|---|---|
| $y$ | | 2 | | | 0.4 |

**(2 marks)**

when $x = 0.5$: $y = \frac{2}{0.5} = $ ......

when $x = 4$:  $y = \frac{2}{4} = $ ......

(b) On the grid, draw the graph of $y = \frac{2}{x}$.

> Join your points with a smooth curve.

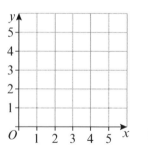

**(2 marks)**

**3** Here are the equations of 4 graphs

A: $y = 2x - 1$     B: $y = \frac{1}{x}$     C: $y = x^2 + 3x - 1$     D: $y = x^3 - 3x^2 + 1$

Write the letter under its matching graph.

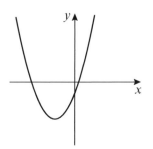 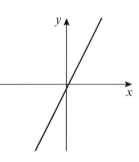 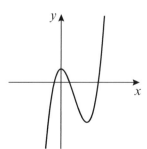 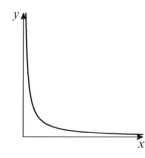

(a) ............     (b) ............     (c) ............     (d) ............

**(2 marks)**

29

# Real-life graphs

1   Bella sells wooden flooring. She uses this graph to work out the cost of flooring.

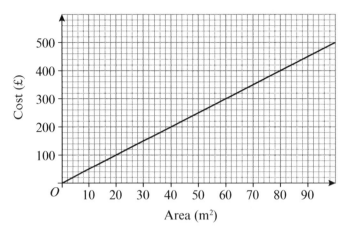

(a)  A floor area is 60 m², how much will it cost?

£......

> Draw a line up from 60 m² to the graph and then across to the cost.

**(1 mark)**

(b)  Another floor costs £350. Use the graph to find its area.

...... m²

> Draw a line across from £350 to the graph and then down.

**(1 mark)**

(c)  How much will a wooden floor cost if it is 5 m wide and 7.4 m long?

Area = ...... × ...... = ...... m²

Cost = £ ......

> Use the graph to find the cost.

**(2 marks)**

2   This graph shows part of Paul's journey to the bank and back.

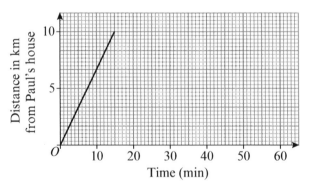

(a)  Work out Paul's speed for the first 15 minutes of his journey. Give your answer in km/h.

Speed = ...... km/h

> If he went 10 km in 15 minutes, he would go ...... km in 60 minutes or 1 hour.

**(2 marks)**

(b)  Paul spends 15 minutes in the bank and then travels back at 20 km/h. Complete the travel graph.

> He travels zero distance while in the bank so the line will be horizontal for 15 minutes. If he travels 20 km in 60 minutes (1 hour), he will travel the return 10 km in ...... minutes.

**(2 marks)**

# Quadratic equations

**1** (a) Solve $x^2 + 8x + 15 = 0$.

$(x + \ldots\ldots)(x + \ldots\ldots) = 0$

Either $x + \ldots\ldots = 0$   or   $x + \ldots\ldots = 0$

So $x = -\ldots\ldots$   or   $x = -\ldots\ldots$

> First factorise.

> If $A \times B = 0$, then either $A = 0$ or $B = 0$.

**(2 marks)**

(b) Solve $x^2 - 2x - 8 = 0$.

$(x - \ldots\ldots)(x + \ldots\ldots) = 0$

Either $x - \ldots\ldots = 0$   or   $x + \ldots\ldots = 0$

So $x = \ldots\ldots$   or   $x = -\ldots\ldots$   **(2 marks)**

(c) Solve $x^2 - 6x + 5 = 0$.

$(x - \ldots\ldots)(x - \ldots\ldots) = 0$

$x = \ldots\ldots$   or   $x = \ldots\ldots$

**(2 marks)**

**2** (a) Solve $x^2 - 7x = -12$.

$x^2 - 7x \ldots\ldots = 0$

$(\ldots\ldots)(\ldots\ldots) = 0$

$x = \ldots\ldots$   or   $x = \ldots\ldots$

> Rearrange to get the quadratic = 0.

> Now factorise.

**(2 marks)**

(b) Solve $6 = x^2 - x$.

> Rearrange.

$\ldots\ldots = 0$

$(\ldots\ldots)(\ldots\ldots) = 0$

$x = \ldots\ldots$ or $x = -\ldots\ldots$

**(2 marks)**

**3** (a) Solve $2x^2 + 5x - 3 = 0$.

$(2x - \ldots\ldots)(x + \ldots\ldots) = 0$

> Work through 'factorising' (page 18) first.

$2x - \ldots\ldots = 0$   or   $x + \ldots\ldots = 0$

$2x = \ldots\ldots$   or   $x = -\ldots\ldots$

$x = \ldots\ldots$   or   $x = \ldots\ldots$

**(2 marks)**

(b) Solve $2x^2 + 7x + 6 = 0$.

$(2x \ldots\ldots)(x \ldots\ldots) = 0$

$2x \ldots\ldots = 0$   or   $x \ldots\ldots = 0$

$2x = \ldots\ldots$   or   $x = \ldots\ldots$

$x = \ldots\ldots$   or   $x = \ldots\ldots$

**(2 marks)**

**4** Find $x$.

> Use Pythagoras' theorem: $(x - 7)^2 + x^2 = (x + 1)^2$.

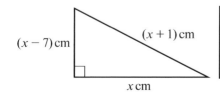

$(x - 7)\,\text{cm}$   $(x + 1)\,\text{cm}$   $x\,\text{cm}$

> You will need to use problem-solving skills throughout your exam – **be prepared!**

> Expand brackets carefully, rearrange to give quadratic = 0, and then solve to find $x$.

**(3 marks)**

# The quadratic formula

**PROBLEM SOLVED!**

**1** Solve $x^2 + 2x - 1 = 0$. Give your solutions to 2 decimal places.

Substitute $a = 1$   $b = 2$   $c = -1$ into the formula.

$$x = \frac{- \ldots \pm \sqrt{\ldots^2 - 4x \ldots \times \ldots}}{2 \times \ldots}$$

$$\boxed{x = \frac{-b \pm \sqrt{b^2 - 4ac}}{2a} \text{ for } ax^2 + bx + c = 0}$$

You will need to use problem-solving skills throughout your exam – **be prepared!**

$$x =$$

$$= \frac{- \ldots \pm \sqrt{\ldots}}{\ldots}$$

$$= \frac{- \ldots \pm \sqrt{\ldots}}{\ldots} \text{ or } \frac{- \ldots - \sqrt{\ldots}}{\ldots}$$

You will get 2 answers, one using the +, and one using the – sign.

$x = \ldots$   or   $\ldots$ to 2 d.p.                    **(3 marks)**

**2** (a) Solve $2x^2 - 4x + 1 = 0$. Give your solutions to 2 decimal places.

$a = \ldots$   $b = \ldots$   $c = \ldots$

Remember – $(-4)$ is $+4$!

$$x = \frac{\ldots \pm \sqrt{\ldots^2 - 4 \times \ldots \times \ldots}}{2 \times \ldots}$$

$$= \frac{\ldots \pm \sqrt{\ldots}}{\ldots}$$

$x = \ldots\ldots\ldots$   or   $\ldots\ldots\ldots$ to 2 d.p.                    **(3 marks)**

(b) Write down the solutions of $4x^2 - 8x + 2 = 0$ to 2 d.p.   Use part (a) to help you.

$\ldots\ldots\ldots$   **(1 mark)**

**3** (a) Solve $3x^2 - 2x - 4 = 0$. Give your solutions to 3 significant figures.

Guided

**PROBLEM SOLVED!**

You will need to use problem-solving skills throughout your exam – **be prepared!**

$x = \ldots\ldots\ldots$   or   $\ldots\ldots\ldots$   **(3 marks)**

(b) Solve $9x^2 - 6x - 12 = 0$. Give your solutions to 3 s.f.

$x = \ldots\ldots\ldots$   or   $\ldots\ldots\ldots$   **(1 mark)**

**4** Solve $2x^2 + x = 5$. Give your answer to 3 s.f.

$2x^2 + x = \ldots\ldots\ldots = 0$

First, rearrange to get all terms on the left-hand side.

$x = \ldots\ldots\ldots$ or $x = \ldots\ldots\ldots$

**(3 marks)**

# Completing the square

**1** Write $x^2 + 4x - 2$ in the form $(x + a)^2 + b$, where $a$ and $b$ are constants.

$(x + \ldots)^2 - \ldots^2 - 2$

$= (x + \ldots)^2 - \ldots$

> The number in front of $x$ divided by 2.

> Simplify last 2 terms.

**(2 marks)**

**2** (a) Write $x^2 - 6x + 1$ in the form $(x + a)^2 + b$.

$(x - \ldots)^2 - \ldots^2 + 1$

$= (x - \ldots)^2 - \ldots$

**(2 marks)**

(b) Hence, write down the minimum value of the curve $y = x^2 - 6x + 1$.

> For the curve $y = (x + a)^2 + b$, the minimum point is $(-a, b)$.

$(\ldots, \ldots)$   **(2 marks)**

**3** (a) Express $x^2 - 8x + 15$ in the form $(x + a)^2 + b$.

$(x \ldots \ldots)^2 \ldots \ldots$   **(2 marks)**

(b) Hence solve $x^2 - 8x + 15 = 0$.

$(x \ldots)^2 \ldots = 0$

$(x \ldots)^2 = \ldots$

$x \ldots = \ldots$   or   $\ldots$

$x = \ldots$   or   $\ldots$

> You will need to use problem-solving skills throughout your exam – **be prepared!**

> Solve.

> Square root.

**(2 marks)**

**4** By completing the square, solve $x^2 - 4x + 2 = 0$.
Give your answers in surd form.

$(x \ldots)^2 \ldots = 0$

$(x \ldots)^2 = \ldots$

$x \ldots = \pm \sqrt{\ldots}$

$x = \ldots$   or   $\ldots$

> You will need to use problem-solving skills throughout your exam – **be prepared!**

> Rearrange to find $x$.

**(3 marks)**

**5** By completing the square, solve $x^2 - 6x + 7 = 0$.
Give your answers in surd form.

...............................   **(4 marks)**

# Simultaneous equations 1

**1** Solve the simultaneous equations.

$2x + y = 11$

$3x - 2y = 13$

$\ldots x + 2y = \ldots$

$\underline{3x - 2y = 13}$

$\ldots x \qquad = \ldots$

$x \qquad = \ldots$

$2 \times \ldots + y = 11$

$y = \ldots$

> Multiply the top equation by 2.

> Now add the 2 equations.

> Substitute the value for $x$ back into the top equation.

> Solve.

**(3 marks)**

**2** Solve the simultaneous equations.

$3x + 4y = -1$

$5x + 2y = -4$

$3x + 4y = -1$

$\ldots x + \ldots y = \ldots$

$\overline{\ldots x \qquad = \ldots}$

$x \qquad = \ldots$

$y = \ldots\ldots\ldots\ldots$

> Mulitiply bottom equation by 2.

> Now subtract.

> Substitute back into either equation to find $y$.

**(3 marks)**

**PROBLEM SOLVED!**

**3** Jon bought 3 cups of tea and 1 cake for £1.90. When he bought 2 cups of tea and 1 cake the cost was £1.40. Work out the cost of a cup of tea, and the cost of a cake.

> You will need to use problem-solving skills throughout your exam – **be prepared!**

$3t + c = 190 \text{ pence}$

$\ldots t + \ldots c = \ldots$

$t = \ldots p \quad c = \ldots p$

> Write as simultaneous equations.

> Now solve.

**(4 marks)**

**4** Tara bought 2 goats and 4 sheep for £240. When she bought 1 goat and 6 sheep the cost was £260. Work out the cost of a goat and the cost of a sheep.

goat = $\ldots\ldots\ldots\ldots$, sheep = $\ldots\ldots\ldots\ldots$

**(4 marks)**

# Simultaneous equations 2

 **5** Solve algebraically the simultaneous equations

$y = x - 2$

$y^2 + x^2 = 10$

$$(x - 2)^2 + x^2 = 10$$

$$(\ldots)(\ldots) + x^2 = 10$$

$$x^2 - \ldots x + \ldots + x^2 = 10$$

$$\ldots x^2 - \ldots x + \ldots = 10$$

$$\ldots x^2 - \ldots x - \ldots = 0$$

$$x^2 - \ldots x - \ldots = 0$$

$$(\ldots)(\ldots) = 0$$

$$x = \ldots \text{ or } x = \ldots$$

When $x = \ldots$, $y = \ldots$

When $x = \ldots$, $y = \ldots$

> Substitute $y = x - 2$ into the 2nd equation.

> Expand and simplify.

> Form a quadratic equation.

> Divide by 2.

> Factorise.

> Solve.

> Substitute these back into $y = x - 2$.

> **Check** that your answers work in the 2nd equation!

**(5 marks)**

 **6** Solve algebraically the simultaneous equations

$x + y = 3$

$y = x^2 - 2x - 3$

$$x^2 - 2x - 3 = \ldots\ldots\ldots\ldots$$

$$\ldots\ldots\ldots\ldots = 0$$

$$(\ldots)(\ldots) = 0$$

$$x = \ldots\ldots\ldots\ldots \text{ or } x = \ldots\ldots\ldots\ldots$$

$$y = \ldots\ldots\ldots\ldots \text{ or } y = \ldots\ldots\ldots\ldots$$

> Rearrange the 1st equation to make $y$ the subject.

> Then put the 2 equations equal to each other.

> Rearrange.

> Factorise and solve.

> Substitute $x$ into 1st equation.

**(4 marks)**

 **7** (a) Here is a graph of the lines
$y = x - 2$ and $x + 2y = 5$.

Using the graph, solve the simultaneous equations

$y = x - 2$

$x + 2y = 5$

 You will need to use problem-solving skills throughout your exam – **be prepared!**

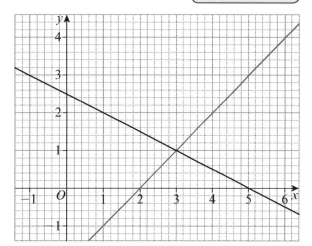

$x = \ldots\ldots\ldots, \, y = \ldots\ldots\ldots$    **(2 marks)**

(b) Solve algebraically these simultaneous equations and compare your answers.

$\ldots\ldots\ldots$    **(3 marks)**

# Equation of a circle

**1** Write down the equation of a circle with

(a) centre (0, 0) and radius 7

$X^2 + y^2 = r^2$

$X^2 + y^2 = \ldots\ldots^2$

$X^2 + y^2 = \ldots\ldots$

> The general equation for a circle with centre (0, 0) is $x^2 + y^2 = r^2$

**(1 mark)**

(b) centre (0, 0) and radius 9

$x^2 + y^2 = \ldots\ldots$

**(1 mark)**

(c) centre (0, 0) and radius 3.5

**(1 mark)**

**2** Write down the centre and radius of the circles with the following equations.

(a) $x^2 + y^2 = 36$

$centre = (0, 0)$

$radius = \sqrt{\ldots\ldots}$

$= \ldots\ldots$

> When the equation is in this form, the centre is always (0, 0) and the radius is the square root of 25.

**(1 mark)**

(b) $x^2 + y^2 = 2.25$

$centre = (\ldots\ldots, \ldots\ldots)$

$radius = \ldots\ldots$

**(1 mark)**

**PROBLEM SOLVED!**

**3** (a) Solve the simultaneous equation algebraically.

$x^2 + y^2 = 25$

$y = 1 - x$

> Substitute $y = 1 - x$ into $x^2 + y^2 = 25$

$x^2 + (1 - x)^2 = 25$

$x^2 + (1 - x)(1 - x) = 25$

$x^2 + \ldots\ldots - x - x + \ldots\ldots^2 = 25$

$x^2 + \ldots\ldots - \ldots\ldots x + \ldots\ldots^2 = 25$

$\ldots\ldots x^2 - \ldots\ldots x - \ldots\ldots = 0$

$x^2 - x - \ldots\ldots = 0$

$(x + \ldots\ldots)(x - \ldots\ldots) = 0$

$x = \ldots\ldots$ and $x = \ldots\ldots$

When $x = \ldots\ldots$ then $y = 1 - \ldots\ldots = \ldots\ldots$

When $x = \ldots\ldots$ then $y = 1 - \ldots\ldots = \ldots\ldots$

> You will need to use problem-solving skills throughout your exam – **be prepared!**

> Expand the bracket.

> Collect like terms.

> Re-arrange to form a quadratic equation.

> Now factorise and solve.

> Substitute the values of $x$ into $y = 1 - x$ to get $y$.

**(5 marks)**

(b) Draw the graph of $x^2 + y^2 = 25$ and $y = 1 - x$ and prove the above solutions graphically.

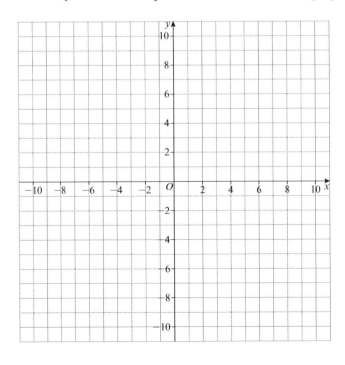

**(4 marks)**

# Inequalities

**1** What integer values of $x$ satisfy these inequalities?

(a) $-1 \leqslant x < 4$   | List all the whole numbers between 4 and –1, including –1. |

(b) $5 \leqslant x \leqslant 8$

$-1, ..., ..., ..., 3$      **(1 mark)**      $..., ..., ..., ...$      **(1 mark)**

**2** Solve these inequalities.

(a) $4x - 1 > 15$

> | Solve inequalities just as if you are solving an equation. |

$4x > ...$    (+1 to both sides)

> | Remember to write your answer as an inequality. |

$x > ...$    (÷ both sides by 4)      **(2 marks)**

(b) $2x + 6 > x + 2$      (c) $5x - 3 \geqslant 2x + 6$

$x + 6 > 2$    $(- x$ from both sides)

$x > ...$      **(2 marks)**      ............      **(3 marks)**

**3** Solve these inequalities.

(a) $-2x + 10 \leqslant 22$ | When you multiply or divide inequalities by a negative number the inequality sign changes direction. |

(b) $28 < 2(-3x - 1)$

$-2x \leqslant ...$

$x \geqslant ...$

     **(2 marks)**      ............      **(3 marks)**

**4** Solve these inequalities.

(a) $\frac{6x - 3}{5} \leqslant 9$

$6x - 3 \leqslant ...$ (× both sides by 5)

$6x \leqslant ...$ (+3 to both sides)

$x \leqslant ...$ (÷ both sides by 6)      **(2 marks)**

(b) $\frac{3x + 1}{2} < \frac{2x - 4}{3}$

     ............      **(3 marks)**

**5** Ben is $x$ years old.
Ali is 3 years older than Ben.
Zeshan is 4 times older than Ali.
The total of all three of their ages is greater than 75.
What is the least value Ben's age could be?

> | You will need to use problem-solving skills throughout your exam – **be prepared!** |

Ben = $x$      Ali = ...      Zeshan = ...      **(5 marks)**

# Quadratic inequalities

**1** Solve these inequalities.

(a) $x^2 - 4 < 0$

$(x + 2)(x - ...) < 0$

> Factorise the left-hand side of this equation.

> Now think about what this quadratic graph looks like.
> The graph would cut the x-axis at 2 and −2.
> The shaded section shows the values of x where the quadratic is less than zero.

This shaded region can be written as

$-2 < x < ...$

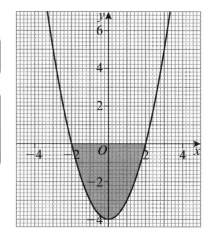

**(2 marks)**

(b) $x^2 - 25 > 0$

$(x + ...)(x - ...) > 0$

> Now think about what this quadratic graph looks like.
> The graph would cut the x-axis at 5 and −5.
> The shaded section shows the values of x where the quadratic is greater than zero.

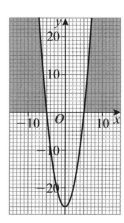

This shaded region can be written as $x < -5$ and $x > ...$     **(2 marks)**

(c) $x^2 - 1 \leqslant 0$

.............     **(2 marks)**

**2** Solve these inequalities.

> A sketch of each graph will help you here.

(a) $x^2 - 3x - 10 \geqslant 0$

$(x - ...)(x + 2) \geqslant 0$

$x \geqslant ...$ and $x \leqslant ...$     **(2 marks)**

(b) $x^2 + 10x + 21 < 0$

$(x + ...)(x + ...) < 0$

$... < x < ...$     **(2 marks)**

(c) $x^2 - 7x + 6 > 0$

.............     **(2 marks)**

**3** Solve $-x^2 - x + 6 \leqslant 0$

> A sketch of the graph will help you here.

> You will need to use problem-solving skills throughout your exam – **be prepared!**

**PROBLEM SOLVED!**

.............     **(3 marks)**

# Trigonometric graphs

**1** (a) Draw the graph of $y = \sin(x)$ in the range $0° \leqslant x \leqslant 360°$

> Use your calculator to find $\sin 90°$, $\sin 180°$, $\sin 270°$ and $\sin 360°$ and plot these points.
> Join the points up with a smooth curve.

> You will need to use problem-solving skills throughout your exam – **be prepared!**

**(2 marks)**

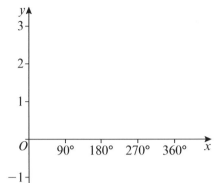

(b) What are the coordinates of the turning points?

Turning point = (..., ...) and (..., ...)   **(2 marks)**

(c) Use the graph above to solve $\sin(x) = 0.5$ in the range $0° \leqslant x \leqslant 360°$

> Draw the line $y = 0.5$
> The solutions are where the line $y = 0.5$ intersects the curve.

$x = $ ......° and $x = $ ......°   **(2 marks)**

(d) Use the graph above to solve $\sin(x) = 2$, what do you notice?   **(1 mark)**

**2** Use your calculator to solve the following equations for $x$, giving your answers in degrees and rounded to 2 decimal places.

(a) $\cos(x) = 0.25$

> To find the first solution use the inverse cos button on your calculator.

$x = \cos^{-1}(0.25) = $ ............. $= $ ......° (2 d.p.)

> Use a sketch of the cos graph and symmetry to find the second solution.

**(2 marks)**

$x = 360° - $ ...... $= $ ......°

(b) $\sin(x) = -0.3$

$x = $ ............. $= $ ......° (2 d.p.)

and

$x = $ ......° $- $ ......° $= $ ......°   **(2 marks)**

**3** (a) Draw the graph of $y = \tan(x)$ in the range $0° \leqslant x \leqslant 360°$

**(2 marks)**

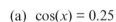

(b) Use the graph above to explain what is happening at $\tan(90°)$ and $\tan(270°)$.

**(2 marks)**

# Transforming graphs

 **1** The graph of $y = f(x)$ is shown on each diagram. Sketch the graph of

(a)  $y = f(x - 1)$        (b)  $y = f(x) - 2$        (c)  $y = 2f(x)$

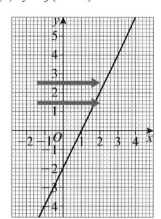    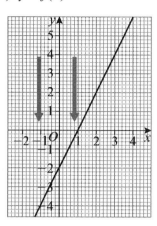   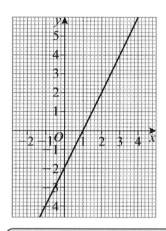

| This is a translation of 1 unit in the positive x-direction. | This is a translation of 2 units in the negative y-direction. | This is a stretch in the y-direction. All y-coordinates are doubled and the x-coordinates stay the same. |

**(2 marks)**        **(2 marks)**        **(2 marks)**

 **2** The point (2, 6) lies on this curve $y = f(x)$. What is the new coordinate after the following transformations?

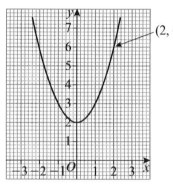

(a)  $y = f(x + 3)$

     (........., .........)  **(2 marks)**

(b)  $y = f(2x)$ ⟵ | This is a squash in the x-direction. All x-coordinates are halved and y-coordinates stay the same. |

     (........., .........)  **(2 marks)**

(c)  $y = -f(x)$ | Reflects graph in the x-axis. |     (d)  $y = f(-x)$ | Reflects graph in the y-axis. |

     (........., .........)  **(1 mark)**        (........., .........)  **(1 mark)**

 **3** The graph of $y = \cos(x)$ is shown for $0° \leqslant x \leqslant 360°$. It has been transformed such that the original coordinate of $(90°, 0)$ is now $(45°, 0)$. What is the possible new equation of the curve after the transformation?

Guided

**PROBLEM SOLVED!**

| You will need to use problem-solving skills throughout your exam – **be prepared!** |  |

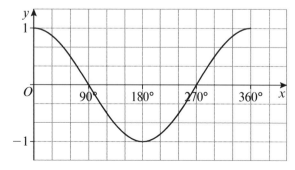

.................................................................................................................................  **(2 marks)**

# Inequalities on graphs

**1** On the grid, shade the region that satisfies all three of these inequalities

$$x \leqslant 5, \qquad y < x \qquad \text{and} \qquad y > -2$$

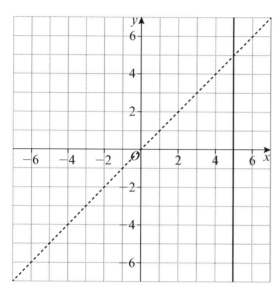

Draw the lines $x = 5$,
$y = x$ and $y = -2$.
< and > lines are dotted and ≤ and ≥
lines are solid.

Now shade in the region which satisfies
all three of the inequalities.
Pick a point in your chosen region
to check if it satisfies all of the
inequalities.

**(4 marks)**

**2 (a)** On the grid, shade the region that satisfies all three of these inequalities

$$x < 1, \qquad y - 2x < 3 \qquad \text{and} \qquad y \geqslant -4$$

You will need to use
problem-solving skills
throughout your exam
– **be prepared!**

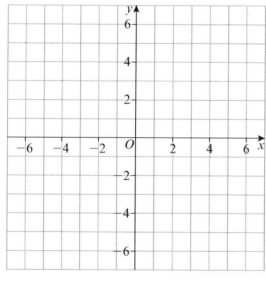

**(4 marks)**

**(b)** Mark with a cross (×) on your grid all the coordinates $(x, y)$, where $x$ and $y$ are
integers, that satisfy these three inequalities.

**(2 marks)**

# Using quadratic graphs

 **1** (a)  Sketch the graph of $y = x^2 + 2x - 1$ in the interval $-4 \leqslant x \leqslant 2$.

> Use a table of values – this might not be given to you in the exam.

> Substitute each $x$-coordinate into each term of the quadratic.

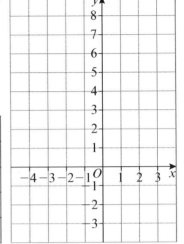

| $x$ | $-4$ | $-3$ | $-2$ | $-1$ | $0$ | $1$ | $2$ |
|-----|------|------|------|------|-----|-----|-----|
| $x^2$ | 16 | 9 | 4 | 1 | …… | …… | …… |
| $+ 2x$ | $-8$ | $-6$ | $-4$ | …… | …… | 2 | 4 |
| $-1$ | $-1$ | $-1$ | $-1$ | $-1$ | $-1$ | $-1$ | $-1$ |
| $y$ | …… | 2 | $-1$ | …… | …… | …… | …… 4 |

> Add up all of your answers to get the $y$-coordinates.

**(4 marks)**

(b)  Use your graph to find estimates to the equation $x^2 + 2x - 1 = 1$

………………

> Draw the line $y = 1$ on your graph. The solutions are where $y = 1$ intersects $y = x^2 + 2x - 1$.

**(2 marks)**

**2** (a)  Construct a table of values (similar to that given in Q1) for $y = x^2 - x + 3$ in the interval $-2 \leqslant x \leqslant 3$ and sketch the corresponding graph in this interval.

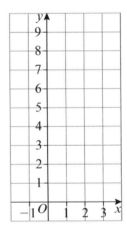

**(4 marks)**

(b)  Use your graph to find estimates to the following equations.

> You will need to use problem-solving skills throughout your exam – **be prepared!**
>

(i)  $x^2 - x + 3 = 4$

………………

**(2 marks)**

(ii)  $x^2 - x = 3$

………………

> What do you need to do to both sides of this equation to make the left-hand side look like the original?

**(2 marks)**

(iii)  $x^2 - x - 2 = 0$

$x^2 - x - 2 + \text{………………} = \text{………………}$

$x^2 - x + 3 = \text{………………}$

$x = \text{………………}$

**(2 marks)**

# Turning points

**1** Find the turning points of these quadratic equations.

> When finding the turning points you need to complete the square.

(a) $y = x^2 + 6x + 7$

$y = (x + \,......)^2 - \,...... + 7$

> The $x$-coordinate of the turning point is always the opposite sign of the number inside the squared bracket. The $y$-coordinate is always the number on the outside of the bracket.

$y = (x + \,......)^2 - \,......$

Turning point $= (-3, -2)$     **(3 marks)**

(b) $y = x^2 + 8x + 22$              (c) $y = x^2 - 2x + 5$

$y = (x + \,......)^2 - \,......+ 22$

$y = (x + \,......)^2 + \,......$

Turning point $= (......, ......)$  **(3 marks)**      Turning point $= (......, ......)$   **(3 marks)**

**2** Find the coordinates of the vertex and state whether the quadratics are a maximum or a minimum.

(a) $y = x^2 - 10x + 16$

> The vertex is another word for turning point.

(b) $y = -x^2 + 6x - 1$

> If the quadratic has a positive $x^2$, then the quadratic is a minimum.

$y = -(x^2 - 6x + 1)$

$y = -((x - \,......)^2 - \,...... + 1)$

$y = -(x - \,......)^2 + \,......$

Vertex $= (......, ......)$   **(4 marks)**

Vertex $= (......, ......)$   **(4 marks)**

**3** (a) Write $y = x^2 + 18x + 120$ in the form $(x + p)^2 + q$, where $p$ and $q$ are integers to be found.

> $(x + p)^2 + q$ means complete the square.

$p = ......$

$q = ......$   **(2 marks)**

(b) Find the turning point of this quadratic equation.

............   **(1 mark)**

(c) What is the equation of the line of symmetry?

> Draw the line of symmetry on a sketch of this quadratic. What equation is this?

............   **(1 mark)**

**4** A quadratic equation has a turning point at $(-2, 5)$.

(a) Find the equation of this quadratic; write your answer in the form $ax^2 + bx + c$.

> You will need to use problem-solving skills throughout your exam – **be prepared!**

............   **(2 marks)**

(b) Describe the transformation from the original equation $y = x^2$

............   **(2 marks)**

43

# Sketching graphs

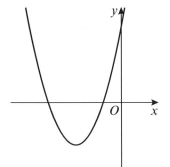

**1** Write down the coordinates where these quadratic equations intercept the $x$-axis and $y$-axis.

(a) $y = x^2 + 5x + 4$

> The graph cuts the $y$-axis when $x = 0$.

$y = 0^2 + 5(0) + 4$

$y = 4$

$y\text{-intercept} = (0, \ldots\ldots)$

$x^2 + 5x + 4 = 0$

> The graph cuts the $x$-axis when $y = 0$.

$(x + 4)(x + 1) = 0$

> Now factorise to get a solution for $x$.

$x = \ldots\ldots$ and $x = \ldots\ldots$

$x\text{-intercept} = (\ldots\ldots, 0)$ and $(\ldots\ldots, 0)$          **(3 marks)**

(b) $y = -x^2 + 2x + 8$

When $x = 0$ then $y = \ldots\ldots$          $y\text{-intercept} = (0, \ldots\ldots)$

When $y = 0$ then $-x^2 + 2x + 8 = 0$

> Move all terms over to the right-hand side to make $x^2$ positive and easier to work with.

$x^2 - 2x - 8 = 0$

$(x - 4)(x + 2) = 0$

> Now factorise.

$x = \ldots\ldots$ and $x = \ldots\ldots$

$x\text{-intercept} = (\ldots\ldots, 0)$ and $(\ldots\ldots, 0)$          **(3 marks)**

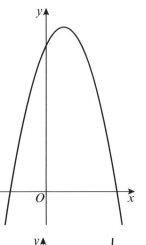

**2** Write down the intercepts these cubic graphs make with the $x$- and $y$-axes.

(a) $y = (x + 1)(x - 2)(x - 3)$

When $x = 0$ then $y = \ldots\ldots$          $y\text{-intercept} = (0, \ldots\ldots)$

When $y = 0$ then $(x + 1)(x - 2)(x - 3) = 0$

$x = \ldots\ldots, x = \ldots\ldots$ and $x = \ldots\ldots$

$x\text{-intercept} = (\ldots\ldots, 0), (\ldots\ldots, 0)$ and $(\ldots\ldots, 0)$          **(4 marks)**

(b) $y = x(x - 5)(x + 2)$

$y\text{-intercept} = (0, \ldots\ldots)$

> Don't forget your third solution here of $x = 0$.

$x\text{-intercept} = (\ldots\ldots, 0), (\ldots\ldots, 0)$ and $(0, 0)$          **(4 marks)**

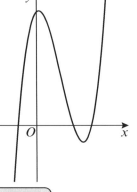

**3** Sketch the following curves, identifying all coordinates where the equations intercept the $x$- and $y$-axes.

(a) $y = x^2 + 2x - 3$

> You will need to use problem-solving skills throughout your exam – **be prepared!**

          **(3 marks)**

(b) $y = (x + 4)(x + 3)(x - 1)$

          **(4 marks)**

(c) $y = -x(x - 2)(x - 6)$

> As the cubic is negative you start drawing the curve 'downhill' rather than 'uphill'.

          **(4 marks)**

# Iteration

1  (a)  Iterate this function $x_{n+1} = \sqrt[3]{2x_n - 3}$ six times. Start with $x_1 = 1$

$x_1 = 1$

$x_2 = \sqrt[3]{2(1) - 3} = -1$

> Keep substituting your answer back in for $x_n$, making sure you write down the full answer on your calculator display.

$x_3 = \sqrt[3]{2(-1) - 3} = \ldots\ldots$

$x_4 = \sqrt[3]{2(\ldots\ldots) - 3} = \ldots\ldots$

$x_5 = \sqrt[3]{2(\ldots\ldots) - 3} = \ldots\ldots$

$x_6 = \sqrt[3]{2(\ldots\ldots) - 3} = \ldots\ldots$        **(2 marks)**

(b)  Comment on your results to part (a).

> What one number is this sequence converging to? Look at where the numbers start to round to the same value.

$x = \ldots\ldots\ldots(2\ d.p.)$        **(1 mark)**

2  (a)  Show that $x^3 - 3x + 4 = 0$ can be rearranged to make $x = \sqrt[3]{3x - 4}$.

$x^3 = 3x - \ldots\ldots$        $x = \overset{\ldots\ldots}{\sqrt{3x - \ldots\ldots}}$        **(2 marks)**

(b)  Use the iterative formula $x_{n+1} = \sqrt[3]{3x_n - 4}$ with $x_1 = 1$ to find a real solution to 2 d.p.

$x_1 = 1$

$x_2 = \sqrt[3]{3(1) - 4} = -1$

$x_3 = \ldots\ldots$

> Keep going until you get the same value to 2 d.p.        **(3 marks)**

3  (a)  Show that $x^3 - 7x + 5 = 0$ can be rearranged to make $x = \dfrac{x^3 - 5}{7}$

        **(2 marks)**

(b)  Use the iterative formula $x_{n+1} = \dfrac{(x_n)^3 - 5}{7}$ with $x_1 = -1$ to find a real solution to 5 d.p.

**(3 marks)**

4  (a)  Use the iterative formula $x_{n+1} = \dfrac{2(x_n)^2 + 2}{5}$ with $x_1 = 1$ to find a real solution to 2 d.p.

$\ldots\ldots\ldots\ldots$        **(3 marks)**

(b)  Below is the graph of $y = x$ and $y = \dfrac{2x^2 + 2}{5}$. What does the solution to part (a) represent on the graph? Annotate this on the graph.

> You will need to use problem-solving skills throughout your exam – **be prepared!**

>  The solution is found where both graphs intersect.

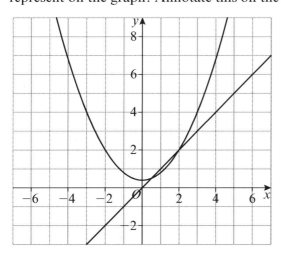

**(1 mark)**

# Rearranging formulae

**1** Rearrange $v = u + at$ to make $a$ the subject.

$v = u + at$ ($-u$ from both sides)

$v - \ldots\ldots = at$ ($\div$ both sides by $t$)

$a = \dfrac{v - \ldots\ldots}{\ldots\ldots\ldots}$

**(2 marks)**

**2** Rearrange $y(x^2 - v) = w$ to make $x$ the subject.

$\ldots\ldots x^2 - \ldots\ldots v = w$ ($+ \ldots\ldots v$ to both sides)

$\ldots\ldots x^2 = w + \ldots\ldots v$ ($\div$ both sides by $\ldots\ldots$)

$x^2 = \dfrac{w + \ldots\ldots}{\ldots\ldots\ldots\ldots}$ ($\sqrt{}$ both sides)

$x = \sqrt{\dfrac{w + \ldots\ldots}{\ldots\ldots\ldots\ldots}}$

> Expand the brackets.

**(3 marks)**

**3** Rearrange $\dfrac{3(4a + b)}{2 - 5ab} = 2$ to make $a$ the subject.

$\dfrac{3(4a + b)}{2 - 5ab} = 2$ ($\times$ both sides by $(2 - 5ab)$)

$3(4a + b) = 2(\ldots\ldots - \ldots\ldots)$ (Expand both brackets)

$12a + 3b = \ldots\ldots - \ldots\ldots ab$

$12a + \ldots\ldots ab = 4 - \ldots\ldots$

> Bring everything with an $a$ onto one side of the equation and everything else onto the other.

$a(\ldots\ldots + \ldots\ldots) = 4 - \ldots\ldots$ ($\div$ both sides by $(\ldots\ldots + \ldots\ldots)$)

$a = \dfrac{4 - \ldots\ldots}{\ldots\ldots + \ldots\ldots}$

> Factorise the left-hand side.

**(4 marks)**

**4** Rearrange $D = \sqrt{\dfrac{e + f}{f + 4e}}$ to make $f$ the subject.

$D = \sqrt{\dfrac{e + f}{f + 4e}}$ (square both sides)

$D^{\ldots\ldots} = \dfrac{e + f}{f + 4e}$       $f = \ldots\ldots\ldots$

**(4 marks)**

**5** Rearrange $\dfrac{1}{u} + \dfrac{1}{v} = \dfrac{1}{f}$ to make $v$ the subject.

> You will need to use problem-solving skills throughout your exam – **be prepared!**

**PROBLEM SOLVED!**

$v = \ldots\ldots\ldots$

**(5 marks)**

# Algebraic fractions

1  Simplify

(a) $\dfrac{1}{2} + \dfrac{3}{4x}$

> Just like adding numerical fractions, you need to make the denominators the same.
> Multiply the first fraction by $2x$, remembering whatever you multiply the denominator by you have to do the same to the numerator.

$\dfrac{(\times\ 2x)}{(\times\ 2x)}\dfrac{1}{2} + \dfrac{3}{4x} = \dfrac{.........}{4x} + \dfrac{3}{4x} = \dfrac{.........}{4x}$    **(2 marks)**

(b) $\dfrac{3}{5x} + \dfrac{7}{2x}$

> What can you multiply each fraction by to make the denominators the same?

$\dfrac{(\times\ 2)}{(\times\ 2)}\dfrac{6}{10x} + \dfrac{......}{......}\ \dfrac{(\times\ ......)}{(\times\ ......)}$

$= \dfrac{......}{10x} =$    **(3 marks)**

(c) $\dfrac{8}{x + 2} - \dfrac{1}{x}$   [Make both denominators $x(x + 2)$.]    (d) $\dfrac{5}{x - 1} - \dfrac{2}{x + 4} =$

$= \dfrac{8x}{x(x + 2)} - \dfrac{............}{x(x + 2)} = \dfrac{............}{x(x + 2)}$  **(3 marks)**        ............    **(3 marks)**

2  Simplify

(a) $\dfrac{5x + 5}{(x + 1)\,(x + 2)}$

> Factorise as much as you can and then simplify.

(b) $\dfrac{3x - 6}{x^2 + 5x - 14}$

$= \dfrac{5(.........)}{(x + 1)\,(x + 2)} = \dfrac{.........}{(x + 2)}$   **(2 marks)**

$= \dfrac{3(.........)}{(x + 7)\,(x - ......)} = \dfrac{......}{......}$

**(3 marks)**

(c) $\dfrac{6x + 18}{x^2 - 9} =$

> Watch out for the 'difference of two squares'.

............

**(3 marks)**

3  Simplify

(a) $\dfrac{5x}{2} \times \dfrac{2}{x}$

$= \dfrac{......}{2x} = \dfrac{......}{......} = ......$

> When you multiply fractions, you multiply the numerators and the denominators.

(b) $\dfrac{x - 1}{x + 2} \times \dfrac{4x + 8}{2x - 2}$    **(2 marks)**

$= \dfrac{x - 1}{x + 2} \times \dfrac{4(......)}{2(......)} = ......$

> Factorise first and simplify.    **(2 marks)**

(c) $\dfrac{6x^3}{5} \div \dfrac{x^2}{15}$

$= \dfrac{6x^3}{5} \times \dfrac{15}{x^2} = \dfrac{......}{5x^2} = ......$

> When you divide fractions, you flip the second fraction and then multiply.

(d) $\dfrac{x^2 - 16}{7x + 14} \div \dfrac{6x + 24}{x + 2} =$

............

**(3 marks)**

4  Simplify

$\dfrac{3x + 6}{x - 1} \times \dfrac{x + 4}{6x - 18} \times \dfrac{2x - 2}{5x + 20} \div \dfrac{x + 2}{5x - 15}$    **(4 marks)**

# Quadratics and fractions

**1** Solve $\dfrac{2-x}{x} = x$

> Multiply each term in the equation by $x$.

$\dfrac{x(2-x)}{x} = x^2$

> Simplify the fraction by cancelling and then rearrange to make a quadratic equation.

$x^2 + x - \ldots\ldots = 0$

> Solve the quadratic equation by factorising.

$(x + \ldots\ldots)(x - \ldots\ldots) = 0$

$x = \ldots\ldots$ and $x = \ldots\ldots$

**(4 marks)**

**2** Solve $\dfrac{5x+3}{2x} = x$

> Multiply each term in the equation by $2x$.

$\ldots\ldots\ldots\ldots$  **(4 marks)**

**3** Solve $9 - \dfrac{40}{2x} = x$

$\ldots\ldots x - \ldots\ldots = 2x^2$

> Multiply each term in the equation by $2x$.

$2x^2 - \ldots\ldots x + \ldots\ldots = 0$

> Divide every term by 2.

$x^2 - \ldots\ldots x + \ldots\ldots = 0$

$(x \ldots\ldots)(x \ldots\ldots) = 0$

$x = \ldots\ldots$ and $x = \ldots\ldots$

**(4 marks)**

**4** Solve $\dfrac{2}{x+1} + \dfrac{3}{x+3} = 1$

> Multiply each term in the equation by the product of the denominators $(x+1)(x+3)$.

$\dfrac{2(x+1)(x+3)}{x+1} + \dfrac{3(x+1)(x+3)}{x+3} = (x+1)(x+3)$

> Simplify the fractions by cancelling and then multiply out the brackets.

$\ldots\ldots x + \ldots\ldots + \ldots\ldots x + \ldots\ldots = x^2 + \ldots\ldots x + \ldots\ldots x + \ldots\ldots$

> Rearrange to make a quadratic equation and solve.

$\ldots\ldots x + \ldots\ldots = x^2 + \ldots\ldots x + \ldots\ldots$

$x^2 - \ldots\ldots x - \ldots\ldots = 0$

$(x + \ldots\ldots)(x - \ldots\ldots) = 0$

$x = \ldots\ldots$ and $x = \ldots\ldots$

**(5 marks)**

**5** Solve $\dfrac{1}{x+1} - \dfrac{1}{x+3} = \dfrac{2}{3}$

$\ldots\ldots\ldots\ldots$  **(5 marks)**

**6** Solve this equation, rounding your final answer to 3 significant figures.

$\dfrac{5}{x+2} + \dfrac{3}{x-1} = 2$

> This equation will not factorise, you will need to use the quadratic formula.

> You will need to use problem-solving skills throughout your exam – **be prepared!**

$\ldots\ldots\ldots\ldots$  **(5 marks)**

48

# Surds 2

**1** Show that $(3 + \sqrt{5})^2 = 14 + 6\sqrt{5}$

$(3 + \sqrt{5})^2 = (3 + \sqrt{5})(......)$

$= 9 + ......\sqrt{5} + ......\sqrt{5} + ......$

$= ...... + ......\sqrt{5}$

> Expand $(3 + \sqrt{5})^2$ as a double bracket.
>
> Remember $\sqrt{a} \times \sqrt{a} = a$

**(2 marks)**

**2** Show that $(2 + 3\sqrt{6})^2 = 58 + 12\sqrt{6}$

$(2 + 3\sqrt{6})^2 = (2 + 3\sqrt{6})(......)$

$= 4 + ......\sqrt{6} + ......\sqrt{6} + ......$

$= ...... + ......\sqrt{6}$

> $3\sqrt{6} \times 3\sqrt{6} = 9 \times 6 = .....$

**(3 marks)**

**3** Expand $(\sqrt{2} - \sqrt{3})^2$

.........

> Remember $\sqrt{a} \times \sqrt{b} = \sqrt{ab}$

**(3 marks)**

**4** Expand and simplify $(3\sqrt{5} - 2\sqrt{7})^2$

$(3\sqrt{5} - 2\sqrt{7})^2 = (3\sqrt{5} - 2\sqrt{7})(......)$

$= ...... - ......\sqrt{35} - ......\sqrt{35} + ......$

$= ...... - ......\sqrt{35}$

**(3 marks)**

**5** Find the values of $p$ and $q$ in

$(p + \sqrt{3})^2 = 19 + q\sqrt{3}$

where $p$ and $q$ are positive integers.

$(p + \sqrt{3})(p + \sqrt{3}) = 19 + q\sqrt{3}$

$p^2 + ...\sqrt{3} + ...\sqrt{3} + ... = 19 + q\sqrt{3}$

$p^2 + ...\sqrt{3} + ... = 19 + q\sqrt{3}$

$p^2 + 3 = ...$ so $p = ...$

and

$q = ...$

> You will need to use problem-solving skills throughout your exam – **be prepared!**
>
> Expand the left–hand side and compare it to the right.

**(4 marks)**

**6** Calculate the area of the trapezium, leaving your answer in surd form.

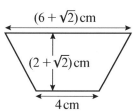

> Area of trapezium $= \frac{1}{2}h(a + b)$ where $a$ and $b$ are parallel sides.
>
> You will need to use problem-solving skills throughout your exam – **be prepared!**

.........   **(3 marks)**

# Functions

**1** If $f(x) = \frac{1}{x}$ where $x \neq 0$ and $g(x) = x^2 + 1$

(a)  Calculate $g(3)$

$g(3) = (3)^2 + 1 = \text{.........}$

> Substitute 3 into $x^2 + 1$.     **(1 mark)**

(b)  Find $f(5)$

$f(5) = \text{.........}$     **(1 mark)**

(c)  Find $fg(x)$

$fg(x) = \dfrac{1}{\text{......}}$

> Start with $g(x)$ and substitute into $f(x)$.     **(1 mark)**

**2** If $f(x) = x^2$ and $g(x) = 5x + 4$

(a)  Find $gf(x)$

$gf(x) = 5\text{.........} + 4$     **(1 mark)**

(b)  Calculate $fg(2)$

$g(2) = 5(\text{......}) + 4 = \text{.........}$

> Calculate $g(2)$ and then substitute into $f(x)$.

$f(\text{......}) = (\text{......})^2 = \text{.........}$     **(2 marks)**

**3** If $f(x) = 2x - 1$ and $g(x) = 3x^2 + 9$

> Guided  ~~X~~

> **PROBLEM SOLVED!**

(a)  Find $g(4)$

> You will need to use problem-solving skills throughout your exam – **be prepared!**

.........     **(1 mark)**

(b)  Solve $f(x) = 11$

.........     **(2 marks)**

(c)  Find $ff(x)$

.........     **(2 marks)**

**4** If $f(x) = \frac{1}{x + 1}$ and $g(x) = \frac{3}{x}$

(a)  Solve $f(x) = g(x)$

$\dfrac{1}{x + 1} = \dfrac{3}{\text{......}}$

> Rearrange to make $x$ the subject.

$x = 3(\text{.........})$

$x = \text{.........}$

$\text{.........}x = \text{.........}$

$x = \text{.........}$     **(3 marks)**

(b)  Solve $gg(x) = 27$

.........     **(2 marks)**

# Inverse functions

**1** The function $f(x) = 5x - 2$

    (a) Find $f^{-1}(x)$

$$y = 5x - 2$$

> Rearrange $y = 5x - 2$ to make $x$ the subject.

$$y + \ldots\ldots = 5x$$

$$x = \frac{y + \ldots\ldots}{\ldots\ldots\ldots}$$

$$f^{-1}(x) = \frac{x + \ldots\ldots}{\ldots\ldots\ldots}$$

> Replace the $y$ with an $x$.

**(2 marks)**

    (b) Calculate $f^{-1}(13)$

> Substitute 13 into your inverse function.

$\ldots\ldots\ldots\ldots$ **(1 mark)**

**2** If $g(x) = \dfrac{4x}{3} + 2$, which of the following would represent $g^{-1}(x)$?

    (a) $g^{-1}(x) = \dfrac{4x}{3} - 4$        (b) $g^{-1}(x) = \dfrac{4x}{2} - 2$        (c) $g^{-1}(x) = \dfrac{3x - 6}{4}$

$\ldots\ldots\ldots\ldots$ **(2 marks)**

**3** If $f(x) = \dfrac{x}{2}$ and $g(x) = \sqrt{x + 9}$

    (a) Find $g^{-1}(x)$                        (b) Solve $g^{-1}(x) = 0$

$$y = \sqrt{x + 9} \qquad\qquad\qquad x^{\cdots} - \ldots = 0$$

$$y^{\cdots} = x + 9 \qquad\qquad\qquad x = \ldots \text{ and } x = \ldots \qquad \textbf{(2 marks)}$$

$$x = y^{\cdots} - \ldots$$

$$g^{-1}(x) = \ldots \qquad \textbf{(2 marks)}$$

    (c) Find $gf^{-1}(8)$

$$f^{-1}(x) = \ldots\ldots\ldots\ldots$$

> Substitute 8 into the inverse of $f(x)$ and then substitute your answer into $g(x)$.

$$f^{-1}(8) = \ldots\ldots\ldots\ldots$$

$$g(\ldots\ldots) = \ldots\ldots\ldots\ldots \qquad \textbf{(3 marks)}$$

**4** If $f(x) = \sqrt{5x}$ and $g(x) = x + 2$

    (a) Find $f^{-1}g^{-1}(x)$

> You will need to use problem-solving skills throughout your exam – **be prepared!**

$\ldots\ldots\ldots\ldots$ **(3 marks)**

    (b) Find $gg^{-1}(x)$

$\ldots\ldots\ldots\ldots$ **(2 marks)**

    (c) Solve $g(x) = f^{-1}(x)$

> Hint: you will need to use the quadratic formula to solve the equation.

$\ldots\ldots\ldots\ldots$ **(3 marks)**

# Algebraic proof

**1** Prove $(2n + 4)^2 - (2n + 1)^2 = 12n + 15$

> Expand the brackets and simplify on the LHS.

$\text{LHS} = (2n + 4)(\ldots\ldots) - (2n + 1)(\ldots\ldots)$

$= 4n^2 + \ldots n + \ldots n + 16 - (4n^2 + \ldots n + \ldots n + 1)$

$= 4n^2 + \ldots n + 16 - (4n^2 + \ldots n + 1)$

$= \ldots n + \ldots = \text{RHS}$                                     **(3 marks)**

**2** Prove that the sum of any 3 consecutive whole numbers is a multiple of 3 for all positive integer values of $n$.

> Consecutive means next to, so use $n$, $n + 1$ and $n + 2$ as three consecutive numbers.

$n + n + 1 + n + 2 = \ldots n + \ldots = \ldots(n + \ldots)$

… can be taken out as a factor so divisible by 3.                **(2 marks)**

**3** Prove that the sum of the squares of three consecutive odd numbers is not divisible by 12, for all positive integer values of $n$.

> Use $2n + 1$, $2n + 3$ and $2n + 5$ as three consecutive odd numbers.

$(2n + 1)^2 + (2n + 3)^2 + (2n + 5)^2$

$= (2n + 1)(\ldots\ldots) + (2n + 3)(\ldots\ldots) + (2n + 5)(\ldots\ldots)$

$= 4n^2 + \ldots n + \ldots n + 1 + 4n^2 + \ldots n + \ldots n + 9 + 4n^2 + \ldots n + \ldots n + 25$

$= 4n^2 + \ldots n + 1 + 4n^2 + \ldots n + 9 + 4n^2 + \ldots n + 25$

$= \ldots n^2 + \ldots n + \ldots$

$= \ldots(n^2 + \ldots n) + \ldots$

… cannot be taken out as a factor of every term so <u>not</u> divisible by 12.   **(4 marks)**

**4** Prove that $(2n - 1)^2 + (2n + 1)^2 - 1$ is not a multiple of 2, for all positive integer values of $n$.

**(3 marks)**

**5** Prove $x^2 + 2x + 2$ is always positive for any value of $x$.

> Complete the square.

$(x + \ldots\ldots)^2 - \ldots\ldots + 2$

$= (x + \ldots\ldots)^2 + \ldots\ldots$

When you square any number and add a number to it you will always get a p…… answer.

> You will need to use problem-solving skills throughout your exam – **be prepared!**

**(3 marks)**

**6** Prove $x^2 + 4x + 7$ is always positive for any value of $x$.

> You will need to use problem-solving skills throughout your exam – **be prepared!**

**(3 marks)**

# Exponential graphs

**1** (a) Plot the graph of $y = 3^x$ in the interval $-3 \leq x \leq 2$.

| $x$ | $-3$ | $-2$ | $-1$ | $0$ | $1$ | $2$ |
|---|---|---|---|---|---|---|
| $y$ | ...... | $0.\dot{1}$ | $0.\dot{3}$ | ...... | ...... | ...... |

**(3 marks)**

(b) Now plot the graph of $y = \left(\frac{1}{3}\right)^x$ in the interval $-2 \leq x \leq 3$ on the same graph.

| $x$ | $-2$ | $-1$ | $0$ | $1$ | $2$ | $3$ |
|---|---|---|---|---|---|---|
| $y$ | ...... | ...... | $1$ | $\frac{1}{3}$ | ...... | ...... |

**(3 marks)**

(c) Describe the relationship between these two graphs.

This is a r...... in the ......-axis

**(2 marks)**

**2** Ronald sketches the graph of $y = \left(\frac{1}{4}\right)^x$ for $x \geq 0$.

Give one reason why the sketch must be incorrect.

................................................................ **(1 mark)**

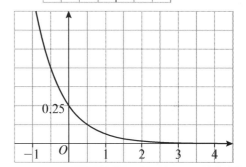

**3** The total attendance for rugby matches is decreasing exponentially by 10%. The initial attendance was 1000 people. Predict the attendance for the fifth rugby match. Round your answer to 3 significant figures.

......... **(3 marks)**

You will need to use problem-solving skills throughout your exam – **be prepared!**

**4** The number of fish in a pond grows exponentially by the formula $N = ab^t$, where $a$ and $b$ are positive constants. The initial number of fish in the pond was 10 000, this increased to 160 000 after 4 years.

You will need to use problem-solving skills throughout your exam – **be prepared!**

(a) Calculate the values of $a$ and $b$

When $t = 0$, $N = $ .........

Substitute these values into the formula.

$ab^0 = 10\,000$

$a = $ .........

When $t = 4$, $N = $ .........

$.........b^{\cdots} = 160\,000$

$b^{\cdots} = $ .........

$b = \sqrt[\cdots]{......}$

$b = $ .........

**(4 marks)**

(b) Approximately, how many years will it take the pond to exceed 1 million fish?

......... $\times$ .........$^t > 1\,000\,000$

.........$^t > 100$

$t = $ ......... years

**(3 marks)**

# Gradients of curves

**1**  This is the graph of $y = x^2 - 5x + 6$.

Estimate the gradient when $x = 4$.

$\text{Gradient} = \dfrac{\text{change in } y}{\text{change in } x} = \dfrac{3}{\text{......}} = \text{.........}$

> The gradient of the tangent at any point is the same as the gradient of the curve at that point.
>
> Draw a tangent at $x = 4$ and find its gradient. A triangle will help you here.

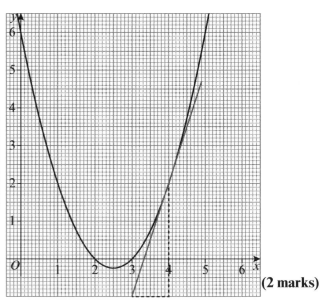

**(2 marks)**

**2**  Olivia throws a ball into the air. The graph shows the vertical height the ball travelled in metres (m), in 4 seconds.

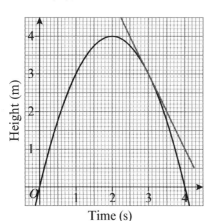

Height (m) / Time (s)

**(a)**  Calculate the average rate of increase of the height between 0 and 2 seconds.

> Draw a chord between $s = 0$ and $s = 2$ and calculate its gradient.

$\text{Gradient} = \dfrac{\text{.......}}{\text{......}} = \text{.........m/s}$     **(2 marks)**

**(b)**  Calculate the average rate of decrease of height at 3 seconds.

> Draw a tangent at $s = 3$ and calculate its gradient.

$\text{Gradient} = \dfrac{\text{.......}}{\text{......}} = \text{.........m/s}$     **(2 marks)**

**3**  This is the graph of $y = e^x$.

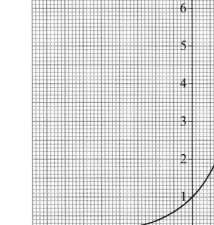

> You will need to use problem-solving skills throughout your exam – **be prepared!**

**(a)**  Estimate the gradient at $x = 0$.

............     **(2 marks)**

**(b)**  Estimate the gradient at $x = 1$.

............     **(2 marks)**

**(c)**  Find the $y$-coordinates when $x = 0$ and $x = 1$. What do you notice?

....................................     **(2 marks)**

# Velocity–time graphs

1   This graph shows the velocity of an object (m/s) for the first 10 seconds of its journey.

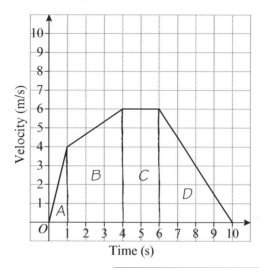

(a)  Work out the acceleration of the object for the first second.

> In this case acceleration is the gradient of the line between 0 and 1 seconds.

$$\text{Acceleration} = \frac{\text{change in } y}{\text{change in } x} = \frac{4}{\ldots\ldots} = \ldots\ldots\ldots \text{m/s}^2$$   **(2 marks)**

(b)  Work out the acceleration of the object in the final 4 seconds.

$$\text{Acceleration} = \frac{\text{change in } y}{\text{change in } x} = \frac{\ldots\ldots}{4} = \ldots\ldots\ldots \text{m/s}^2$$

> Notice there is negative gradient here.

**(2 marks)**

(c)  Work out the total distance travelled by the object.

Area of triangle $A$ = .........
Area of trapezium $B$ = .........
Area of rectangle $C$ = .........
Area of triangle $D$ = .........
Total area = .........
Distance travelled = .........m

> Distance is the area under the graph. Split the shape up into triangles, trapeziums and rectangles and calculate the total area.

**(3 marks)**

2   This graph shows the velocity (m/s) of an object for 3 seconds of its journey.

> You will need to use problem-solving skills throughout your exam – **be prepared!**

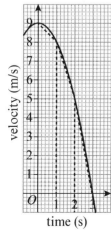

(a)  Estimate the acceleration at $t = 5$.

............   **(2 marks)**

(b)  Estimate the distance travelled by the object.

> The best shapes to use here are trapeziums and triangles. This will not give you an exact area, hence the estimate. The more shapes you can split it up into the better.

............   **(3 marks)**

# Areas under curves

**1** This is the graph of $y = x^2 + 5x$.

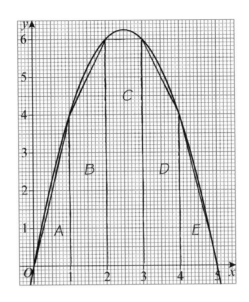

(a) Use five equal intervals to calculate an estimate for the area between the curve and the $x$-axis.

$\text{Area of } A = \frac{1}{2} \times (1 \times 4) = 2$

$\text{Area of } B = \frac{1}{2} \times 1 \times (4 + 6) = \ldots\ldots$

$\text{Area of } C = \ldots\ldots \times \ldots\ldots = \ldots\ldots$

$\text{Area of } D = \frac{1}{2} \times \ldots\ldots \times (\ldots\ldots + \ldots\ldots) = \ldots\ldots$

$\text{Area of } E = \frac{1}{2} \times (\ldots\ldots \times \ldots\ldots) = \ldots\ldots$

$\text{Total Area} = \ldots\ldots$

> The curve above has been split up into 5 equal intervals, labelled *A, B, C, D* and *E*. Calculate each area separately and then find the total area.

**(4 marks)**

(b) Is this estimate an underestimate or overestimate? Give reasons for your answer.

................................................................................................ **(1 mark)**

**2** This graph shows the velocity (km/h) of an object with time, $t$.

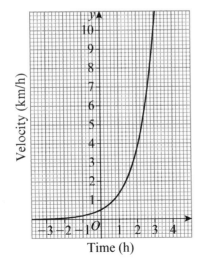

Time (h)

(a) Use three equal intervals to find the area between the curve and the $x$-axis between $t = 0$ and $t = 3$

......................................................... **(4 marks)**

(b) Is this estimate an underestimate or overestimate? Give reasons for your answer.

......................................................... **(1 mark)**

(c) Interpret your result for part (a).

......................................................... **(1 mark)**

> You will need to use problem-solving skills throughout your exam – **be prepared!**

# Problem-solving practice 1

**1**

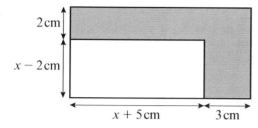

The shaded area is 27.5 cm².

Find the length and width of the smaller rectangle.

27.5 = 2(x +.........)+.........(x − 2)

27.5 = 2x +.........+......... x − .........

27.5 = ......... x + .........

.........x = .........

x = .........

> Split the shaded area into 2 rectangles and find expressions of their areas in terms of *x*.

> Form an equation for the total area and solve it to find *x*.

length = ... cm, width = ... cm　**(4 marks)**

**2**

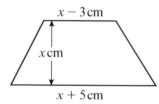

The area of the trapezium is 56 cm².

(a) Show that $x^2 + x − 56 = 0$

> use $A = \frac{1}{2}(a + b)h$

**(3 marks)**

(b) Find the height of the trapezium.

(x ...)(x ...) = 0

x = ... or x = ...

> Solve $x^2 + x − 56 = 0$ by factorising.

> x must be positive.

............　**(3 marks)**

**3** Find the lengths of the sides of this right-angled triangle.

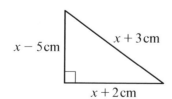

> Use Pythagoras' theorem to form an equation.

............　**(4 marks)**

# Problem-solving practice 2

**4** A car accelerates from rest at a constant rate for 30 seconds to 20 m/s. It then stays at a constant speed for 3 minutes and then decelerates at a constant rate to rest in 10 seconds.

(a) Draw this velocity–time graph.

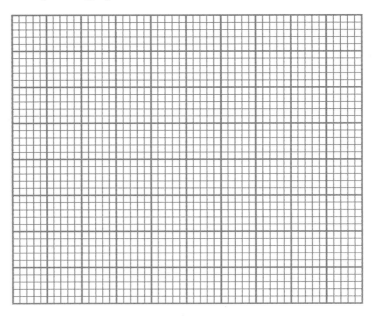

**(3 marks)**

(b) Calculate the deceleration for the last 10 seconds of the car journey.

Deceleration = ………… m/s² **(2 marks)**

(c) Calculate the total distance travelled.

Distance = ………… m **(2 marks)**

**5** Solve $\dfrac{2x + 1}{x + 2} + \dfrac{3x}{x + 1} = 12$, giving your answers to 2 decimal places.

$x =$ ………… and $x =$ ………… **(5 marks)**

**6** Alexandra is $x$ years old.

David is Alexandra's age squared.

Mary is 1 year younger than Alexandra.

The total of all of their ages is greater than 7. What is the greatest age Alexandra could be?

………… **(4 marks)**

# Calculator skills 2

1  Calculate 7% of 23 000 people.

23 000 × ...... = ......

> Write 7% as a decimal and multiply this by 23 000.

**(1 mark)**

2  A dress was originally worth £85. In a sale, there is a 20% discount.
   Calculate the new price of the dress.

£85 x 0.8 = £......

> The multiplier for a 20% decrease is 0.8 (100% − 20% = 80%).

**(2 marks)**

3  Simon invested £500 into a bank with an interest rate of 5% per year.
   Calculate how much money Simon will have in his bank account after 1 year.

£500 x ...... = £......

**(2 marks)**

4  A toy was £28 after a 70% decrease.
   Calculate the price before the sale.

£28 ÷ ...... = £......

> When calculating a reverse percentage you divide by the multiplier instead of multiply.

**(2 marks)**

5  In 2016 an iPod was worth £125 and in 2017 its new price is £105.

   (a) What is the change in price from 2016 to 2017?

Gu~~ided~~ >

**ROBLEM OLVED!**

> You will need to use problem-solving skills throughout your exam – **be prepared!**

**(1 mark)**

   (b) Calculate the percentage decrease from 2016 to 2017.

> Write your answer to part (a) as a percentage of £125.

**(2 marks)**

6  Louisa is travelling around Europe. The exchange rate is £1 = €1.19409

   (a) If she has £20, how much is this in €?

Gu~~ided~~ >

**ROBLEM OLVED!**

> You will need to use problem-solving skills throughout your exam – **be prepared!**

**(1 mark)**

   (b) If she has €7, how much is this in £?

**(2 marks)**

# Ratio

**1** Divide £60 in the ratio 7 : 5.

Total parts = 7 + 5 = ........

1 part = £60 ÷ ......... = £.........

7 parts = 7 × ......... = £........

5 parts = 5 × ......... = £........

> Always begin by adding up the total number of parts.

> Find the value of one part by dividing by the total number of parts.

> Multiply each side of the ratio by the value of one part.

> You know you are correct if your answers add up to the original amount.

**(2 marks)**

**2** In total, there are 240 pupils in Years 7, 8 and 9. The year groups are in the ratio 3 : 5 : 7, respectively. How many pupils are in Year 8?

> Guided

> The question tells you the order of the ratio, so Year 8 has 5 parts.

............   **(2 marks)**

**3** Matt and Gabby are brother and sister. Their heights are in the ratio 5 : 4. Matt's height is 180 cm. What is Gabby's height?

5 parts = 180 cm

1 part = 180 cm ÷ 5 = ........ cm

4 parts = 4 × ......... = ......... cm

**(2 marks)**

**4** Asif and Skye share their money in the ratio 7 : 3. Asif has £48 more than Skye.

(a) Show that Skye has £36.

7 − 3 = 4 parts

4 parts = £48

1 part = £48 ÷ ......... = .........

3 parts = 3 × ......... = .........

> You will need to use problem-solving skills throughout your exam – **be prepared!**

> £48 must be 4 parts as Asif has 4 parts more than Skye.

**(3 marks)**

(b) How much money do they have altogether?

Total money = £............   **(2 marks)**

# Proportion

**1**  The recipe to make 8 scones needs:

350 g self-raising flour                    85 g butter

¼ teaspoon salt                             3 tablespoons caster sugar

1 teaspoon baking powder                    175 ml milk

   (a)  (i)  If Paula wants to make 48 scones, how much butter will she need?

$\times 6 \Big($ 8 scones need 85 g butter

         ↳ 48 scones need 85 × ......... = ......... g of butter

> What do you need to multiply the recipe by?

**(2 marks)**

     (ii)  How much salt will she need?

¼ × ......... = ......... teaspoons                          **(1 mark)**

   (b)  (i)  If she only wants to make 12 scones, how much flour will she need?

$\times .........\Big($ 8 scones need 350 g flour

         ↳ 12 scones need 350 × ......... = ......... g flour             **(2 marks)**

     (ii)  How much baking powder does she need?

......... teaspoons     **(1 mark)**

**2**  Desks are arranged in an exam hall in 15 rows of 12. If the desks were rearranged into 10 rows, how many desks would be in each row?

Total number of desks = ......... × ......... = .........

> How many desks are there in total?

So, new number of desks in each row = ......... ÷ 10

                       = ......... desks

**PROBLEM SOLVED!**

> You will need to use problem-solving skills throughout your exam – **be prepared!**

**(2 marks)**

**3**  It will take 4 bricklayers 6 days to build a large wall. One bricklayer hurts her back and cannot work, how many days will it now take to build the wall?

> You will need to use problem-solving skills throughout your exam – **be prepared!**

**Guided**

**PROBLEM SOLVED!**

......... **(2 marks)**

**4**  If 24 chocolate bars cost £13.68, how much do 7 chocolate bars cost?

......... **(2 marks)**

# Percentage change

**1** A dress is reduced by 30% in a sale. Before the sale the dress costs £80. How much does it cost in the sale?

Discount = $\frac{30}{100}$ × ......... = £ .........

Sale price = 80 − ......... = £ .........

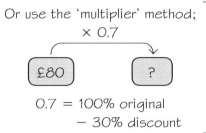

Or use the 'multiplier' method;

× 0.7

£80   →   ?

0.7 = 100% original
    − 30% discount

**(2 marks)**

**2** Joe's car has depreciated in value over the last 5 years by 45%. He bought it 5 years ago for £7000. How much is it worth now?

'Depreciates' means 'goes down in value'.

You will need to use problem-solving skills throughout your exam – **be prepared!**

......... **(2 marks)**

**3** Tara sells an antique vase and makes a profit of 22%. She bought the vase for £84. How much does she sell the vase for?

Profit = $\frac{22}{100}$ × ......... = £ .........

Selling price = ......... + ......... = £.........

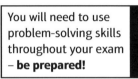

Or use the 'multiplier' method;

× 1.22

£84   →   ?

1.22 = 100% original
     + 22% profit

**(2 marks)**

**4** In a physics experiment, a metal rod is heated and its length increases from 150 cm to 151.5 cm. Find the percentage increase.

Percentage change = $\frac{......}{150}$ × 100

Percentage change = $\frac{\text{change}}{\text{original}}$ × 100

= .........% **(2 marks)**

**5** In a sale, a pencil case has been reduced from £8 to £6.80. Find the percentage discount.

Change = .........

Percentage change = $\frac{......}{......}$ × 100 = .........% **(2 marks)**

**6** In its first 3 weeks, a baby's weight has increased from 4 kg to 4.6 kg. Find the percentage increase in weight.

......... **(2 marks)**

# Reverse percentages

1   In a sale, a television has been reduced by 20% to £480. Find the price of the television before the sale.

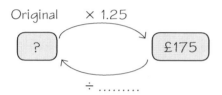

Original    × 0.8    Sale price

? → £480

÷ ..........

0.8 = 100% original
   − 20% discount

**Original** price = £480 ÷ .......... = £..........                                   **(2 marks)**

2   Jody sells some sweets at a fair stall and makes a profit of 25%. Her takings that day are £175. How much had she spent on sweets to sell?

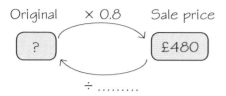

Original    × 1.25

? → £175

÷ ..........

1.25 = 100% original
    + 25% profit

**Original** price = £175 ÷ .......... = £..........                                   **(2 marks)**

3   Paula's sports car has depreciated in value by 35% since she bought it. It is now worth £78 000. How much did she pay for it?

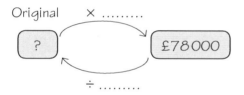

Original    × ..........

? → £78 000

÷ ..........

.............. **(2 marks)**

4   Rita's house has risen in value by 80% in the last 10 years. It is now worth £630 000. How much was it worth 10 years ago?

Gu~~id~~ed

.............. **(2 marks)**

5   The population of Brazil in 2017 was $2.11 \times 10^8$. This was a 21% growth since 2000. What was the population in 2000? Give your answer to 3 significant figures.

You will need to use problem-solving skills throughout your exam – **be prepared!**

Gu~~id~~ed

**ROBLEM
OLVED!**

.............. **(3 marks)**

Had a go ☐  Nearly there ☐  Nailed it! ☐

# Growth and decay

**1** Jordan invests £2000 in a Building Society at an interest rate of 2.3% per annum for 5 years. How much will Jordan have in his account at the end of 5 years?

The total after 1 year will be £2000 × 1.023

100% original
+ 2.3% interest

The total after 2 years will be £(2000 × 1.023) × 1.023

= £2000 × 1.023·····

So the total after 5 years will be £2000 × 1.023·····

= £ ............ **(3 marks)**

**2** The population of a city $t$ years after the year 2000 is given by $P_t$, where $P_0 = 2$ million.

$$P_{t+1} = 1.08\, P_t$$

(a) What is the population of the city at the beginning of 2000?

$t = 0$

............ **(1 mark)**

(b) What is the population of the city at the beginning of 2003?

$P_o = 2$ million

$P_1 = 1.08 × 2$ million = ............

$P_2 = 1.08 × ............ = ............$

$P_3 = ............ × ............ = ............$ **(3 marks)**

**3** In a biology experiment, the number of bacteria in a flask are being studied. The number of bacteria $B$, after $t$ days is given by: $B = 1000 × 1.3^t$

 Guided

(a) What is the initial number of bacteria in the flask?

............ **(1 mark)**

**PROBLEM SOLVED!**

(b) What is the daily percentage increase?

You will need to use problem-solving skills throughout your exam – **be prepared!**

............ **(1 mark)**

(c) Work out the number of bacteria in the flask after 10 days.

............ **(2 marks)**

**4** A car depreciates by 15% each year. The original price of the car was £40000. How much is it worth after 6 years?

**PROBLEM SOLVED!**

£40000 × 0............····· = £ ............

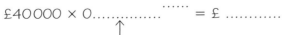

100% original
−15% decrease

You will need to use problem-solving skills throughout your exam – **be prepared!**

**(3 marks)**

# Speed

**1** A car travelled 200 km in 4 hours. Calculate the average speed of the car.

$Speed = Distance ÷ Time$

$Speed = 200 ÷ \ldots\ldots = \ldots\ldots km/h$

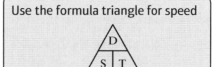
Use the formula triangle for speed

Always remember units on the end of your answers.

**(2 marks)**

**2** A motorbike travels on a motorway at an average speed of 70 km/h for 2 hours. How far was this journey?

$Distance = \ldots\ldots × \ldots\ldots = \ldots\ldots km$

**(2 marks)**

**3** A plane travels 1400 km in $3\frac{1}{2}$ hours. What was the average speed of the plane?

Convert $3\frac{1}{2}$ hours into a decimal.

$\ldots\ldots$ **(2 marks)**

**4** A ship travelling at an average speed of 20 mph covered a distance of 85 miles. How long was the journey in minutes?

$Time = \ldots\ldots ÷ 20 = \ldots\ldots$

$= \ldots\ldots minutes$

**(3 marks)**

**5** An insect crawls 30 cm across the floor in 1 minute. What is the insect's average speed in cm/s?

$1 minute = \ldots\ldots seconds$

$Speed = \ldots\ldots ÷ \ldots\ldots = \ldots\ldots cm/s$

**(3 marks)**

**6** Chloe ran 100 m in 30.3 seconds and Charlie ran 400 m in 75.4 seconds. Who had the faster average speed? Show your working.

$Chloe: Speed = \ldots\ldots ÷ \ldots\ldots = \ldots\ldots m/s$

$Charlie: Speed = \ldots\ldots ÷ \ldots\ldots = \ldots\ldots m/s$

$Faster runner = \ldots\ldots$

**(3 marks)**

**7** A rocket covers a distance of 5000 km in 1 minute. How fast is it travelling in m/s?

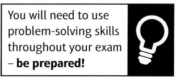
You will need to use problem-solving skills throughout your exam – **be prepared!**

$\ldots\ldots$ **(3 marks)**

# Density

1  The volume of a rectangular brick is 50 cm³.
   The density of the brick is 10 grams per cm³.
   Calculate the mass of the brick.

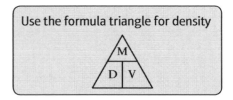
Use the formula triangle for density

Mass = Density × Volume

Mass = ......... × .........

    = ......... grams                                      **(2 marks)**

2  A box of books has a mass of 420 grams.
   The density of the box is 5 grams per cm³.
   **Guided**  Calculate the volume of the box.

                                            .........   **(2 marks)**

3  The density of a rectangular container filled with water is 2.5 kg per m³.
   The container has dimensions 10 m by 12 m by 8 m.
   Calculate the mass of the full container in kg.

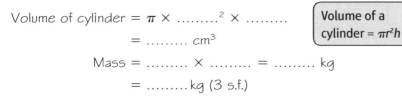

Volume of cuboid = ......... × ......... × ......... = ......... m³

            Mass = ......... × .........

                = ......... kg

Volume of a cuboid = length × width × height          **(3 marks)**

4  The diagram shows a solid cylinder. It has radius 2 cm and a height of 6 cm.
   The density of the cylinder is 1.5 kg per cm³.
   Calculate the mass of the cylinder. Round your answer to 2 s.f.

Volume of cylinder = π × .........² × .........

        = ......... cm³

    Mass = ......... × ......... = ......... kg

      = ......... kg (3 s.f.)

Volume of a cylinder = $\pi r^2 h$

2 cm

6 cm

**(3 marks)**

5  Water is stored in a cylindrical container. The cylinder has
   diameter 250 cm and the depth of the water reaches 130 cm.

**Guided**

**PROBLEM SOLVED!**

  (a)  If 1 litre = 1000 cm³, calculate how many litres of water are in
   the container.
   Give your answer to the nearest litre.

You will need to use problem-solving skills throughout your exam – **be prepared!**
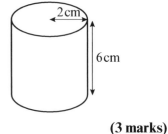

                                    .........   **(3 marks)**

  (b)  The water is poured into 2-litre cans.
   The mass of an empty can is 500 g and the density of the water is 3.5 grams per cm³.
   Calculate the mass of a 2-litre can when full of water.

                                    .........   **(3 marks)**

# Other compound measures

**1** A wardrobe exerts a force of 750 N on the floor.
The base of the wardrobe has area 2.5 m².
Calculate the pressure exerted on the floor.

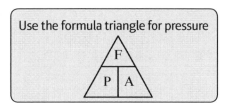
Use the formula triangle for pressure

Pressure = Force ÷ Area

Pressure = ......... ÷ ......... = ......... N/m²      **(2 marks)**

**2** A crate exerts a force of 1300 N on a table.
The pressure on the table is 100 N/cm².
Calculate the area in cm², of the crate on the table.

Area = ......... ÷ ......... = ......... cm²      **(2 marks)**

**3** A suitcase exerts a force of 60 N on the floor.
The pressure on the floor is 120 N/m².
Calculate the area in cm², of the suitcase on the floor.

Area = ......... ÷ ......... = ......... m²

Remember 1 m² = 10 000 cm²

......... × 10 000 = ......... cm²      **(3 marks)**

**4** A rectangular package is resting on a coffee table.
The pressure exerted on the coffee table is 55 N/cm².

Gu~~ided~~

Calculate the force exerted on the coffee table.

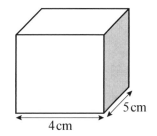
5 cm
4 cm

.........      **(3 marks)**

ROBLEM
OLVED!

**5** A cylindrical can is placed on a shelf. The pressure exerted on the shelf is 42 N/m².

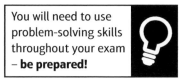
You will need to use problem-solving skills throughout your exam – **be prepared!**

(a) Calculate the force exerted by the can on the shelf. Round your answer to the nearest newton.

Area of cross-section = $\pi r^2$

$= \pi \times$ .........² = ......... m²

Force = ......... × ......... = ......... N

= ......... N (nearest newton)

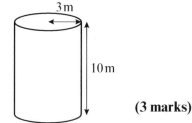
3 m
10 m

**(3 marks)**

(b) A similar cylindrical can is placed on the shelf. This can still exerts 42 N/m² on the shelf but has a force of 21 000 N.
Calculate the radius of the cylinder in metres. Round your answer to 1 d.p.

.........      **(3 marks)**

# Proportion and graphs

**1** This is a conversion graph between pounds and euros.

(a) Use the graph to change £20 to euros.

£20 ≈ ........ euros

> Go to £20 on the *x*-axis. Draw a line up to the conversion line and then straight across to the *y*–axis. What is this value?

**(1 mark)**

(b) Use the graph to change 35 euros to pounds.

35 euros ≈ £ ........

> ≈ means approximately.

> This time go to 35 euros on the *y*-axis. Draw a line across to the conversion line and down to the *x*-axis. What is this value?

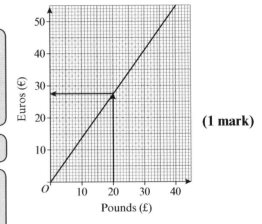

**(1 mark)**

**2** This is a conversion graph between centimetres and inches.

(a) Use the graph to convert 4 inches into centimetres.

4 inches ≈ ........ cm  **(1 mark)**

(b) Use the graph to convert 13 centimetres into inches.

13 cm ≈ ........ inches  **(1 mark)**

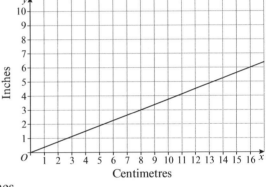

(c) Use the graph to convert 40 centimetres into inches.

4 cm ≈ ........ inches

40 cm ≈ ........ inches

> Find 4 cm in inches and multiply this answer by 10.

**(2 marks)**

(d) What evidence is there from the graph that centimetres are directly proportional to inches?

> Does one quantity increase as the other increases by the same amount each time?

............

**(1 mark)**

**3** The conversion between miles and kilometres is 5 miles ≈ 8 kilometres.

(a) Use this conversion to complete the table.

> You will need to use problem-solving skills throughout your exam – be prepared!

| Miles, m | 0 | 5 | 10 | 20 | 50 | 100 |
|---|---|---|---|---|---|---|
| Kilometres, km | ...... | ...... | ...... | ...... | ...... | ...... |

**(2 marks)**

PROBLEM SOLVED!

Gui**d**ed

(b) On the grid, draw a conversion graph between miles and kilometres.

**(2 marks)**

(c) Use your graph to convert 50 kilometres into miles.

............  **(1 mark)**

(d) Convert 160 miles into kilometres.

............  **(1 mark)**

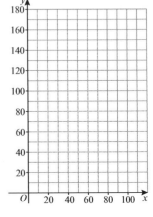

# Proportionality formulae

**1**  $y$ is directly proportional to $x$.

(a) Express $y$ in terms of $x$.

$y \propto x$

$y = ...x$

> The direct proportion formula is always in the form $y = kx$, where $k$ is a constant to be found.

**(1 mark)**

(b) If $y = 28$ and $x = 7$, find the value of the constant $k$.

$y = kx$

$28 = k \times ...$

$k = 28 \div ...$

$k = ...$

**(2 marks)**

(c) Find the value of $y$ when $x = 12$.

$y = kx$

> Substitute $x = 12$ and your value for $k$ into this formula.

$y = ... \times 12$

$y = ...$

**(1 mark)**

**2**  $y$ is directly proportional to $x$ and $y = 70$ when $x = 5$.

(a) Find the value of $y$ when $x = 6$.

$y \propto x$

$y = kx$

$... = k \times 5$

$k = ... \div 5 = ...$

Now, $y = ... \times 6$

$y = ...$

> You will need to find the value of $k$ first.

**(3 marks)**

(b) Find the value of $x$ when $y = 56$.

$y = kx$

$54 = ... \times x$

$x = 54 \div ...$

$x = ...$

**(2 marks)**

**3**  $w$ is inversely proportional to $z$.

(a) Express $w$ in terms of $z$.

$w \propto \frac{1}{z}$

$w = \dfrac{k}{......}$

> The inverse proportion formula is always in the form $y = \frac{k}{z}$, where $k$ is a constant to be found.

**(1 mark)**

(b) If $w = 50$ when $z = 2$, find the value of $w$ when $z = 25$.

$w = \dfrac{k}{z}$

$50 = \dfrac{......}{2}$

$k = ... \times 2$

$k = ...$

Now $w = \dfrac{......}{25}$

$w = ...$

> You will need to find the value of $k$ first.

**(3 marks)**

**4**  In a spring, the tension ($T$ newtons) is directly proportional to the extension ($x$ cm). When the tension is 160 newtons, the extension is 8 cm. Calculate the tension, in newtons, when the extension is 11 cm.

........... **(3 marks)**

> You will need to use problem-solving skills throughout your exam – **be prepared!**

**5**  The number of miles ($M$ miles) a car travels is inversely proportional to the tread depth ($d$ mm) of its tyres. When $M = 120$ then $d = 0.5$ mm. Calculate the tread depth of the tyres after the car has travelled 500 miles.

........... **(3 marks)**

> You will need to use problem-solving skills throughout your exam – **be prepared!**

# Harder relationships

**1** $t$ is directly proportional to the square of $p$.

(a) Express $t$ in terms of $p$.

$$t \propto p^2$$
$$t = \ldots p^2$$

**(1 mark)**

(b) If $t = 75$ when $p = 5$ then find $t$ when $p = 4$.

$$t = kp^2$$
$$\ldots = k \times 5^2$$
$$k = \ldots \div 5^2$$
$$k = \ldots$$
$$\text{so } t = \ldots \times 4^2$$
$$t = \ldots$$

> You will need to find the value of $k$ first.

> Now substitute $p = 4$ and your value for $k$ into the formula to find $t$.

**(3 marks)**

(c) If $t = 27$, find the positive value of $p$.

$$t = kp^2$$
$$27 = \ldots \times p^2$$
$$p^2 = 27 \div \ldots$$
$$p^2 = \ldots$$
$$p = \sqrt{\ldots\ldots}$$
$$p = \ldots$$

**(3 marks)**

**2** $m$ is inversely proportional to the square root of $n$.

If $m = 20$ when $n = 4$ then find the value of $n$ when $m = 10$.

$$m \propto \frac{1}{\sqrt{n}}$$
$$m = \frac{\ldots\ldots}{\sqrt{\ldots\ldots}}$$
$$20 = \frac{k}{\sqrt{\ldots\ldots}}$$
$$k = 20 \times \sqrt{\ldots\ldots}$$
$$k = \ldots$$

$$\text{Now, } 10 = \frac{\ldots\ldots}{\sqrt{n}}$$
$$10 \times \sqrt{n} = \ldots$$
$$\sqrt{n} = \frac{\ldots\ldots}{10}$$
$$\sqrt{n} = \ldots$$
$$n = \ldots^2$$
$$n = \ldots$$

> You will need to find the value of $k$ first.

> Now substitute $m = 10$ and your value for $k$ into the formula to find $n$.

**(4 marks)**

**3** The distance ($D$ cm) travelled by a ball is directly proportional to the cube of the time ($t$ seconds). If $D = 30$ when $t = 50$, find the value of $D$ when $t = 10$.

 **PROBLEM SOLVED!**

> You will need to use problem-solving skills throughout your exam – **be prepared!**

............ **(3 marks)**

**4** The number of hours ($h$ hours) needed to dig a hole is inversely proportional to the square of the number of people ($p$ people) digging it. It takes 4 people 5 hours to dig a hole. If the same hole took 20 hours to dig, how many people were digging?

 **PROBLEM SOLVED!**

> You will need to use problem-solving skills throughout your exam – **be prepared!**

............ **(4 marks)**

# Problem-solving practice 1

1  Jonathan wants to invest some money for 3 years. He wants to maximise his investment.

| Account A | Account B |
|---|---|
| 8.5% interest paid at the end of 3 years | 3% per annum compound interest |

Which account should he use? You must show your working.

Account A:   $x \times 1.085 = \ldots\ldots x$

Account B:   $x \times 1.03^{\ldots\ldots} = \ldots\ldots x$

So Account ......... is better.                                    **(3 marks)**

2  A market trader bought 400 apples and 800 bananas to sell on his stall. He then discovered that 12% of the apples and 15% of the bananas were rotten. What percentage of the fruit was ready for sale?

Number of rotten apples = ......... × 400 = .........

Number of rotten bananas = ......... × 800 = .........

Total rotten fruit = ......... + ......... = .........

Total fresh fruit = 1200 − ......... = .........

Percentage fruit ready for sale = $\frac{\ldots\ldots}{1200} \times 100 = \ldots\ldots\%$          **(3 marks)**

3  A clothing store has a sale where everything is reduced by 30%. On the last day of the sale, a sign in the window announces '20% off all sale prices today'. Ben says 'Great, it's now 50%!'. Explain why he is not correct.

Guided

.................................................................................................................

.................................................................................................................

.................................................................................................................

.................................................................................................................          **(3 marks)**

4  A bouncy ball is dropped from a height. Each time it bounces back up, it reaches 80% of its previous height.

Guided

How many bounces does it take for the ball to bounce to less than half of its original height?

........... **(3 marks)**

# Problem-solving practice 2

**5** A camel travels 60 000 m in 1200 minutes. Calculate its average speed in km/h.

.............. **(3 marks)**

**6** Karen invests £700 on 1st January 2017 at a compound interest rate of $I$% per annum.

The total £$T$, of this investment is given by

$T = 700 \times (1.05)^n$

(a) Calculate the value of the interest $I$.

.............. **(1 mark)**

(b) Calculate the value of $T$ after 10 years.

.............. **(2 marks)**

(c) Calculate the smallest value $n$ could be, in years, if $700 \times (1.05)^n > 1000$.

.............. **(3 marks)**

**7** $a$ is directly proportional to the cube of $b$. When $a = 512$, $b = 2$.

(a) Find the value of the constant.

.............. **(2 marks)**

(b) Calculate the value of $a$ if $b = 3$.

.............. **(2 marks)**

(c) Calculate the value of $b$ if $a = 4096$.

.............. **(2 marks)**

# Angle properties

1   Find *a* and *b*.

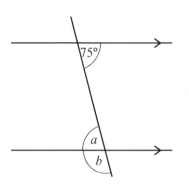

$a = 75°$

$b = 105°$

Alternate angles are equal.

Angles on a straight line add up to 180°.

**(2 marks)**

2   Find *x* and *y*, giving reasons for your answers.

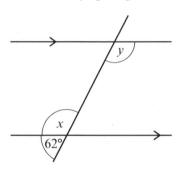

$x = 118°$ because angles on a straight line

add up to 180°

$y = 118°$ because ~~opp~~ alternate angles are equal.

→ denotes parallel lines.

**(4 marks)**

3   Find *a*, *b* and *c*, giving reasons for your answers.

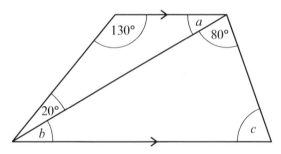

You will need to use problem-solving skills throughout your exam – **be prepared!**

$c = 50°$

$b + a = $ alternate

$a = $

$c = 50°$ because opposite angles in a parrelelogram $= 180°$

All add to 260°   360 - 280 = 80   80/2 = 40

$a = 40°$   $b = 40°$ because alternate angles $= $ ~~180~~ are equal.   **(6 marks)**

4   *ABCD* is a kite. Find angle *BCD*, giving your reasons.

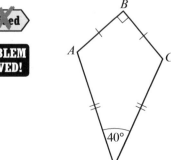

+ denotes equal length.

You will need to use problem-solving skills throughout your exam – **be prepared!**

$+\begin{array}{r}40\\90\\\hline130\end{array}$

.......... **(3 marks)**

# Solving angle problems

**1** Find $x$.

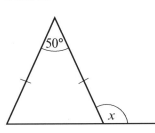

The sum of the base angles

$= 180 - \text{.........} = \text{......}^{\circ}$

So 1 angle $= \text{.........} \div 2 = \text{......}^{\circ}$

So $x = 180 - \text{.........} = \text{......}^{\circ}$

> Angles in a triangle add up to 180°.

**(3 marks)**

**2** Find the angles $x$, $y$ and $z$, giving reasons.

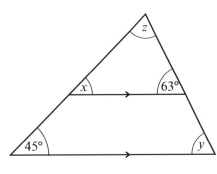

$x = \text{......}^{\circ}$ because corresponding angles

     are ..........................

$y = \text{......}^{\circ}$ because ..........................

     ..........................................

$z = \text{......}^{\circ}$ because angles in a triangle

     add up to $\text{......}^{\circ}$

**(6 marks)**

**3** Find the angles $x$, $y$ and $z$, giving reasons.

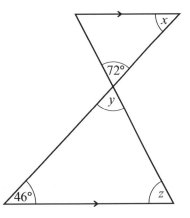

> Alternate angles are equal.

You will need to use problem-solving skills throughout your exam – **be prepared!**

..........................................

..........................................

..........................................

..........................................

..........................................

> Vertically opposite angles are equal.

**(6 marks)**

**4** Find angle $a$, giving your reason.

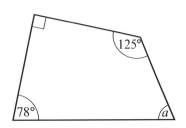

You will need to use problem-solving skills throughout your exam – **be prepared!**

..........................................

..........................................

**(2 marks)**

# Angles in polygons

**1** Find the exterior angle of a regular polygon with 15 sides.

Exterior angle = $\frac{\ldots\ldots}{\ldots\ldots}$ = .......°

> Sum of exterior angles = 360°

**(2 marks)**

**2** Find the number of sides of a regular polygon whose exterior angle is 30°.

Number of sides = $\frac{\ldots\ldots}{\ldots\ldots}$ = ............

**(2 marks)**

**3** Find the interior angle of a regular decagon.

Sum of interior angles = $(n - 2) \times 180°$ where $n$ is the number of sides.

$\qquad = (\ldots\ldots - 2) \times 180°$

$\qquad = \ldots\ldots°$

> A decagon has 10 sides.

So each interior angle = $\frac{\ldots\ldots}{\ldots\ldots}$ = ......°

**(3 marks)**

**4** Find the interior angle of a regular octagon.

 Guided

............   **(3 marks)**

**5** Find the number of sides of a regular polygon whose interior angle is 165°.

Exterior angle = 180° − ............ = ......°

Number of sides = $\frac{\ldots\ldots}{\ldots\ldots}$ = ............

**(3 marks)**

**6** The interior angle of a regular polygon is 5 times bigger than its exterior angle.
How many sides does the polygon have?
Let the exterior angle be $x°$.

> You will need to use problem-solving skills throughout your exam – **be prepared!**

The interior angle is ............$x°$

$x + \ldots\ldots x = 180°$

> exterior + interior = 180°

$\qquad x = \ldots\ldots°$

Number of sides = $\frac{\ldots\ldots}{\ldots\ldots}$ = ............

**(4 marks)**

**7** The interior angle of a regular polygon is 9 times bigger than its exterior angle.
How many sides does the polygon have?

Guided

............   **(4 marks)**

# Pythagoras' theorem

**1**  Find $x$.

Give your answer to 3 significant figures.

$$\underline{...7...}^2 + \underline{...11...}^2 = x^2 \qquad \boxed{a^2 + b^2 = c^2}$$

$$\underline{...49... + 121...} = x^2$$

$$\underline{...170...} = x^2$$

$$x = \sqrt{170} = \underline{..13.0..} \text{ m}$$

$\begin{array}{r} 11 \\ \times 11 \\ \hline 11 \\ 110 \\ \hline 120 \end{array}$   $\begin{array}{r} 121 \\ +\ 49 \\ \hline 170 \end{array}$

**(2 marks)**

**Guided**

**2**  Find $y$, giving your answer to 1 decimal place.

8.2 cm

9.3 cm

$y$

.............   **(2 marks)**

**3**  Find $a$. Give your answer to 1 decimal place.

$$a^2 + \underline{........}^2 = \underline{........}^2$$

$$a^2 = \underline{........}^2 - \underline{........}^2 = \underline{........}$$

$$a = \sqrt{\underline{......}} = \underline{........} \text{ cm}$$

11 cm

$a$

15 cm

**(2 marks)**

**4**  Find the length $CD$. Give your answer to 1 decimal place.

**PROBLEM SOLVED!**

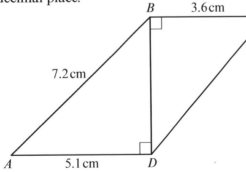

$B$   3.6 cm   $C$

7.2 cm

$A$   5.1 cm   $D$

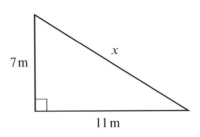
You will need to use problem-solving skills throughout your exam – **be prepared!**

Find $BD$ using Pythagoras in $\triangle ABD$.

Now find $CD$ using Pythagoras in $\triangle BCD$.

Keep all figures in for $BD$ to keep accuracy.

$$BD = \underline{...........} \text{ cm}$$

$$CD = \underline{...........} \text{ cm} \qquad \textbf{(4 marks)}$$

**Guided**

**PROBLEM SOLVED!**

**5**  Is this triangle right-angled? Show your method clearly.

Use numbers in your reason.

You will need to use problem-solving skills throughout your exam – **be prepared!**

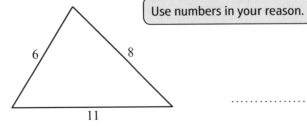

6   8

11

.................................................................

.................................................................

**(2 marks)**

76

# Trigonometry 1

**1** Find angle $x$.

………… $x = \dfrac{\cdots\cdots}{\cdots\cdots}$

$x = \cdots\cdots^{-1}(\cdots\cdots)$

$= \cdots\cdots°$ (to 1 decimal place)

| Label sides Opp., Adj. and Hyp. |
| Choose sin, cos or tan. |

$S_H^o \quad C_H^A \quad T_A^o$

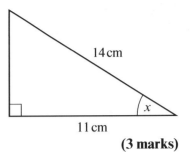

14 cm

11 cm

$x$

**(3 marks)**

Guided

**2** Find angle $y$, giving your answer to 1 decimal place.

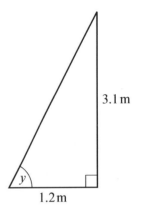

3.1 m

$y$

1.2 m

………… **(3 marks)**

**3** Find the length $x$, giving your answer to 3 significant figures.

………… $28° = \dfrac{\cdots\cdots}{\cdots\cdots}$

$x = \cdots\cdots × \cdots\cdots 28°$

$= \cdots\cdots$ cm

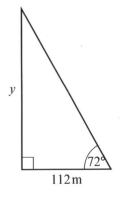

$x$

13 cm

28°

**(3 marks)**

**4** Find length $y$, giving your answer to the nearest metre.

………… $72° = \dfrac{\cdots\cdots}{\cdots\cdots}$

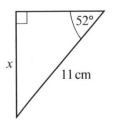

$y$

112 m

72°

$y = \cdots\cdots$ m    **(3 marks)**

Guided

**5** Find $x$.

52°

$x$

11 cm

**(3 marks)**

# Trigonometry 2

**6** Find the length $x$, giving your answer to 1 decimal place.

$$\ldots\ldots 35° = \frac{opp}{hyp} = \frac{\ldots\ldots}{x}$$

$$x = \frac{\ldots\ldots\ldots}{\ldots\ldots 35°} = \ldots\ldots m$$

$$S_H^O \qquad C_H^A \qquad T_H^O$$

Rearrange to make $x$ the subject.

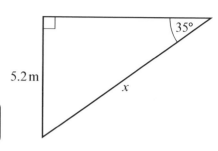

**(3 marks)**

**7** Find the length $a$, giving your answer to 3 significant figures.

$$\ldots\ldots 67° = \frac{\ldots\ldots}{\ldots\ldots}$$

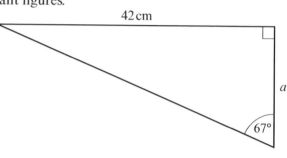

$a = \ldots\ldots$ cm   **(3 marks)**

**8** A flagpole has 2 ropes securing it. Find the angle that the rope $CD$ makes with the ground.

**PROBLEM SOLVED!**

First, find BD, the height of the flagpole in $\triangle ABD$.

You will need to use problem-solving skills throughout your exam – **be prepared!**

$$\ldots\ldots 73° = \frac{BD}{\ldots\ldots}$$

$$So \quad BD = \ldots\ldots cm.$$

$$\ldots\ldots y° = \frac{\ldots\ldots}{\ldots\ldots}$$

Now find $y$, using $\triangle BCD$.

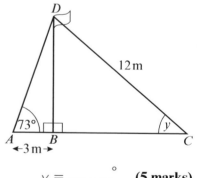

$y = \ldots\ldots °$   **(5 marks)**

**9** Find angle $x$, giving your answer to 1 decimal place.

Guided

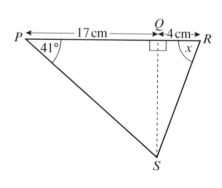

$\ldots\ldots$   **(4 marks)**

# Solving trigonometry problems

**1** $\triangle ABC$ is isosceles. Find its perpendicular height, $h$.

$$\tan 58° = \frac{h}{BC \div 2} = \frac{h}{\ldots\ldots}$$

> Draw a vertical line from $A$ to the midpoint of the base.

$h = \ldots\ldots \times \ldots\ldots = \ldots\ldots$ cm

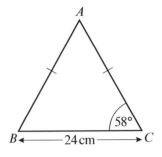

**(3 marks)**

**2** The angle of elevation of $D$ from $B$ is $43°$.
The angle of elevation of $D$ from $A$ is $37°$.
If $BC$ is $8\,$m, find $AB$ to 1 decimal place.

**PROBLEM SOLVED!**

> You will need to use problem-solving skills throughout your exam – **be prepared!**

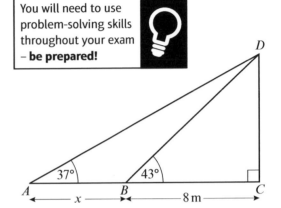

$$\text{Tan } 43° = \frac{CD}{\ldots\ldots}$$

> First, find $CD$, using trigonometry in $\triangle BCD$.

$\quad$ So $CD = \ldots\ldots \times \ldots\ldots$

$\qquad\qquad = \ldots\ldots$ m

Now use $\triangle ACD$:

$$\text{Tan } 37° = \frac{\ldots\ldots}{AC}$$

> Do not round to 1 d.p. here, to keep accuracy.

$\quad AC = \ldots\ldots$ m

So $AB = \ldots\ldots - \ldots\ldots = \ldots\ldots$ m

**(5 marks)**

**3** Find $\angle DBC$.

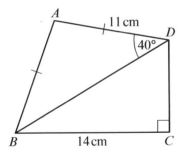

> First, draw in line from $A$ to midpoint of $BD$, to make a right-angled triangle.

> You will need to use problem-solving skills throughout your exam – **be prepared!**

**Guided**

**PROBLEM SOLVED!**

$\ldots\ldots$ ° **(5 marks)**

**4** What is the angle of depression of the boat, at A, from the man standing at the top of the cliff at B?

**Guided**

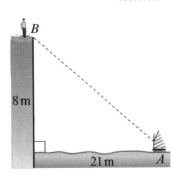

$\ldots\ldots$ **(2 marks)**

# Perimeter and area

**1** Here is a floorplan of Ginny's new bedroom.
Find the area and the perimeter of the room.

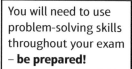 

You will need to use problem-solving skills throughout your exam – **be prepared!**

$2 + 3 + b =$ ...........

So $b =$ ......... m

> First, find the missing lengths $a$ and $b$.

$4 + 2 - a =$ .........   So, $a =$ ......... m

Perimeter = ......... m

> Perimeter is the distance around the shape.

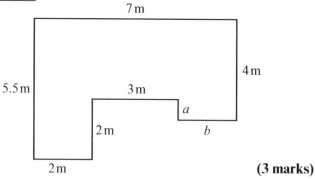

**(3 marks)**

> To find area, split the room into 3 rectangles.

Area A = ......... × ......... = ......... m²

Area B = ......... × 3.5 = ......... m²

Area C = ......... × ......... = ......... m²

Total area = ................................ m²

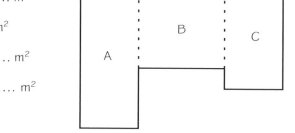

**(4 marks)**

**2** Find the area of the trapezium $ABCD$.

> Draw a line vertically down from A to DC.

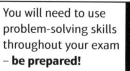

You will need to use problem-solving skills throughout your exam – **be prepared!**

$Dx^2 + 4^2 =$ .........²

$Dx =$ ......... cm     > Use $A = \frac{1}{2}(a + b)h$

So $CD =$ ......... cm.

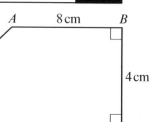

Area = ........... cm²   **(5 marks)**

**3** (a) Find the shaded area of this square.

........... units²   **(3 marks)**

(b) Find the perimeter of the shaded shape.
Leave your answer in surd form.

You will need to use problem-solving skills throughout your exam – **be prepared!**

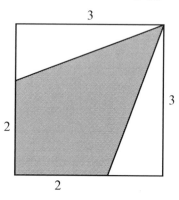

......... $\sqrt{10}$ + .........   **(3 marks)**

# Units of area and volume

**1** Change $3.5\,\text{m}^2$ to $\text{cm}^2$.

$1\,\text{m}^2 = 100 \times 100\,\text{cm}^2 = \ldots\ldots\ldots\ \text{cm}^2$

So $3.5\,\text{m}^2 = 3.5 \times \ldots\ldots\ldots = \ldots\ldots\ldots\ \text{cm}^2$

100 cm

$1\,\text{m}^2$   100 cm

1 km = 1000 m
1 m = 100 cm
1 cm = 10 mm

**(2 marks)**

**2** Change $2.7\,\text{km}^2$ to $\text{m}^2$.

$1\,\text{km}^2 = 1000 \times 1000\,\text{m}^2 = \ldots\ldots\ldots\ \text{m}^2$

So $2.7\,\text{km}^2 = 2.7 \times \ldots\ldots\ldots = \ldots\ldots\ldots\ \text{m}^2$

**(2 marks)**

**3** Change $1.3\,\text{m}^3$ to $\text{cm}^3$.

$1\,\text{m}^3 = 100 \times 100 \times 100\,\text{cm}^3 = \ldots\ldots\ldots\ \text{cm}^3$

So $1.3\,\text{m}^3 = 1.3 \times \ldots\ldots\ldots = \ldots\ldots\ldots\ \text{cm}^3$

**(2 marks)**

**4** Change $2\,500\,000\,\text{cm}^3$ to $\text{m}^3$.

$2\,500\,000 \div \ldots\ldots\ldots = \ldots\ldots\ldots\ \text{m}^3$

**(2 marks)**

**5** Change

(a) $7200\,\text{mm}^3$ to $\text{cm}^3$

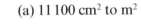

............   **(2 marks)**

(b) $21\,\text{cm}^3$ to $\text{mm}^3$

............   **(2 marks)**

(c) $3.7\,\text{m}^3$ to $\text{cm}^3$.

............   **(2 marks)**

**6** Change

(a) $11\,100\,\text{cm}^2$ to $\text{m}^2$

> Guided

............   **(2 marks)**

(b) $8.2\,\text{km}^2$ to $\text{m}^2$

............   **(2 marks)**

(c) $25.3\,\text{cm}^2$ to $\text{mm}^2$.

............   **(2 marks)**

**7** The scale on a map is 1:50 000

(a) Calculate the actual distance in kilometres between two villages that are 4.2 cm apart on the map.

**PROBLEM SOLVED!**

$4.2 \times \ldots\ldots\ldots = \ldots\ldots\ldots\text{cm}$

$= \ldots\ldots\ldots\text{m}$

$\ldots\ldots\ldots\text{km}$

You will need to use problem-solving skills throughout your exam – **be prepared!**

**(2 marks)**

**PROBLEM SOLVED!**

(b) The area of an actual forest is $730\,000\,\text{m}^2$. Calculate the area of the forest on the map in $\text{cm}^2$.

You will need to use problem-solving skills throughout your exam – **be prepared!**

$\ldots\ldots\ldots\ \text{cm}^2$   **(3 marks)**

# Prisms

**1** Find the volume of this triangular prism.

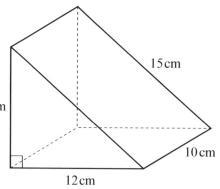

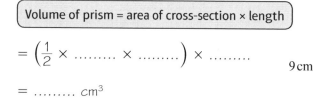
Volume of prism = area of cross-section × length

$$= \left(\frac{1}{2} \times \ldots\ldots \times \ldots\ldots\right) \times \ldots\ldots$$

$$= \ldots\ldots \text{ cm}^3$$

15 cm

9 cm

10 cm

12 cm

**(3 marks)**

**2** Find the total surface area of the triangular prism in question 1.

Total surface area = 2 × area of ◺ + area of 3 rectangles.

$$= 2 \times \left(\frac{1}{2} \times \ldots\ldots \times \ldots\ldots\right) + (\ldots\ldots \times \ldots\ldots) + (\ldots\ldots \times \ldots\ldots) + (\ldots\ldots \times \ldots\ldots)$$

$$= \ldots\ldots + \ldots\ldots + \ldots\ldots + \ldots\ldots$$

$$= \ldots\ldots \text{ cm}^2$$

**(3 marks)**

**3** Find the volume of the trapezoidal prism.

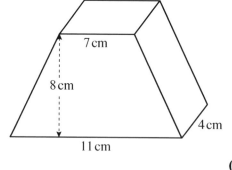

Volume = area of trapezium × length

$$= \frac{1}{2}(a + b)h \times \text{length}$$

$$= \left(\frac{1}{2}(\ldots\ldots + \ldots\ldots) \times \ldots\ldots\right) \times \ldots\ldots$$

$$= \ldots\ldots \times \ldots\ldots$$

$$= \ldots\ldots \text{ cm}^3$$

7 cm

8 cm

11 cm

4 cm

**(3 marks)**

**4** Work out the volume and the total surface area of this prism.

Guided

**PROBLEM SOLVED!**

You will need to use problem-solving skills throughout your exam – **be prepared!**

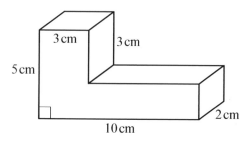

3 cm   3 cm

5 cm

10 cm

2 cm

..............

..............   **(5 marks)**

# Circles and cylinders

**1** Find the area and circumference of this circle.

| Area = $\pi r^2$ |

$\pi \times \dots\dots^2 = \dots\dots\ cm^2$

| Circumference = $2\pi r$ |

$2\pi \times \dots\dots = \dots\dots\ cm$

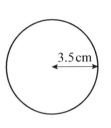

3.5 cm

**(4 marks)**

**2** Find the radius of a circle whose area is $50\ cm^2$.
Give your answer to 1 d.p.

$\pi r^2 = 50 \qquad so \qquad r^2 = \dfrac{50}{\dots\dots}$

$r = \dots\dots\ cm$

**(2 marks)**

**3** Find the volume of this cylinder.

| Volume = $\pi r^2 h$ |

$= \pi \times \dots\dots \times \dots\dots$

$= \dots\dots\ cm^3$

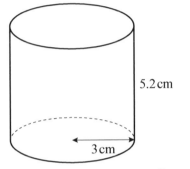

5.2 cm

3 cm

**(2 marks)**

**4** Find the total surface area of the cylinder in question 3.

$= 2\pi rh \qquad\qquad\qquad + 2 \times \pi r^2$

$= 2 \times \pi \times \dots\dots \times \dots\dots + 2 \times \pi \times \dots\dots^2$

$= \dots\dots + \dots\dots$

$= \dots\dots\ cm^2$

You will need to use problem-solving skills throughout your exam – **be prepared!**

**ROBLEM OLVED!**

| Total surface area = curved surface area + 2 × area of circle. |

**(3 marks)**

**5** A stool is in the shape of a solid cylinder; the diameter of the base is 22 cm and the height is 50 cm. Find the total surface area and the volume of the stool.

You will need to use problem-solving skills throughout your exam – **be prepared!**

**Gui̶ded**

**ROBLEM SOLVED!**

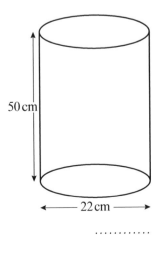

50 cm

22 cm

$\dots\dots\dots$

$\dots\dots\dots$ **(5 marks)**

# Sectors of circles

1  Find the area of this sector.

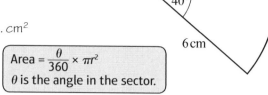

$$\text{Area} = \frac{\text{......}}{360°} \times \pi \times \text{......}^2 = \text{........ cm}^2$$

Area $= \frac{\theta}{360} \times \pi r^2$
$\theta$ is the angle in the sector.

40°

6 cm

**(2 marks)**

2  Find the length of the arc of the sector in question 1.

$$\text{length of arc} = \frac{\theta}{360} \times 2\pi r$$
$$= \frac{\text{......}}{360} \times 2 \times \pi \times \text{........} = \text{........ cm}$$

**(2 marks)**

3  (a)  Find the area of this sector.

 Guided

95°

8 cm

............  **(2 marks)**

(b)  Find the length of the arc in this sector.

............  **(2 marks)**

4  (a)  Find the area of this sector.

Guided

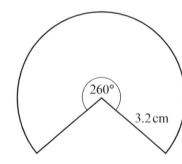

............  **(2 marks)**

260°

3.2 cm

(b)  Find the perimeter of this sector.

Perimeter = length of arc + 2 × radius

............  **(3 marks)**

Guided

PROBLEM SOLVED!

5  The arc length of this sector is 6 cm.
Find the area of the sector.

Find the angle first.

You will need to use problem-solving skills throughout your exam – **be prepared!**

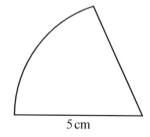

5 cm

............  **(4 marks)**

# Volumes of 3D shapes

**1** Find the volume of a hemisphere with radius 3 cm.

$$= \frac{1}{2} \times \frac{4}{3} \times \pi \times \ldots\ldots\ldots^3 = \ldots\ldots\ldots \text{ cm}^3$$   Volume = $\frac{1}{2}$ of $\frac{4}{3}\pi r^3$

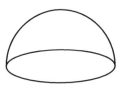

**(2 marks)**

**2** Find the volume of a cone whose height is 11 cm and diameter is 6 cm.

$$= \frac{1}{3} \times \pi \times \ldots\ldots\ldots \times \ldots\ldots\ldots$$

Volume = $\frac{1}{3}\pi r h$

$r$ = diameter ÷ 2

$$= \ldots\ldots\ldots\ldots \text{ cm}^3$$

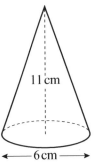

11 cm

6 cm

**(2 marks)**

**3** Find the volume of this square-based pyramid whose height is 8 cm.

Volume = $\frac{1}{3}$ × area of base × height

$$= \frac{1}{3} \times \ldots\ldots\ldots^2 \times \ldots\ldots\ldots$$

$$= \ldots\ldots\ldots \text{ cm}^3$$

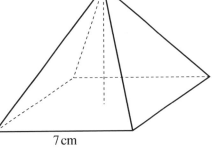

7 cm

**(2 marks)**

**4** A metal solid consists of a hemisphere joined to a cone. 10 of these are melted down to form a cube. What is the length of the side of this cube? Give your answer to 1 decimal place.

**Guided** ✗

**PROBLEM SOLVED!**

First, find the height of the cone using Pythagoras.

You will need to use problem-solving skills throughout your exam – **be prepared!**

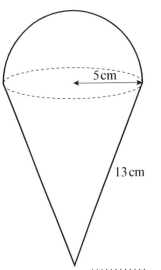

5 cm

13 cm

............ **(6 marks)**

**5** Find the volume of this pyramid whose base is an equilateral triangle of side 6 cm. The height of the pyramid is 9 cm. Leave your answer in surd form.

**Guided** ✗

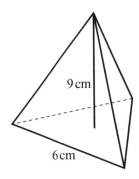

9 cm

6 cm

............ **(4 marks)**

# Surface area

**1** Find the total surface area of this cone.

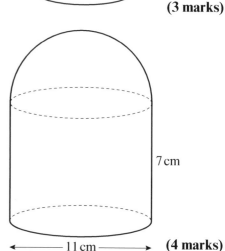

Total surface area = curved surface area + area of circle

$= \pi r l + \pi r^2$     $l^2 = 12^2 + 3^2$

$= \pi \times$ ......... $\times$ ......... $+ \pi \times$ .........$^2$

$=$ ......... $+$ ......... $=$ ......... cm$^2$

**(3 marks)**

**PROBLEM SOLVED!**

**2** Find the total surface area of a solid made from a hemisphere and a cylinder.

Total surface area $= \frac{1}{2} \times 4\pi r^2 + 2\pi r h + \pi r^2$

$= \frac{1}{2} \times 4 \times \pi \times ...^2 + 2 \times \pi \times ... \times ... + \pi \times ...^2$

$=$ ......... $+$ ......... $+$ ......... $=$ ......... cm$^2$

You will need to use problem-solving skills throughout your exam – **be prepared!**

7 cm

11 cm   **(4 marks)**

**3** Find the total surface area of this square-based pyramid.

Total surface area = area of base + 4 × area of Δ

(height of Δ)$^2 + 5^2 = 12^2$

So height of Δ, $h =$ ......... cm

12 cm

10 cm

Total surface area $=$ .........$^2 + 4 \times \left( \frac{1}{2} \times \text{.........} \times \text{.........} \right)$

$=$ ......... $+ 4 \times$ ......... $=$ ......... cm$^2$

**(5 marks)**

**4** Find the total surface area of a frustum formed when a small cone, radius 2 cm, has been removed from a larger cone, radius 4 cm.

**Guided**

**PROBLEM SOLVED!**

You will need to use problem-solving skills throughout your exam – **be prepared!**

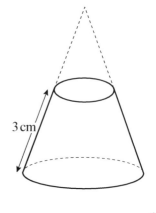

3 cm

............   **(5 marks)**

# Plans and elevations

**1** A model is made out of 5 cubes.

(a) On the grid below, draw the elevation of the model from the direction shown by the arrow.

**(2 marks)**

(b) On the grid below, draw the plan of the model.

The plan describes the shape from above.

**(2 marks)**

**2** Here are the plan and front elevation of a prism.

plan        front elevation

(a) On the grid below, draw the side elevation.

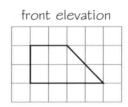

**(2 marks)**

(b) What is the name of this type of prism?

............ **(1 mark)**

**3** The diagram shows a solid made from 10 cubes.

Complete the plan view of the solid on the grid below.

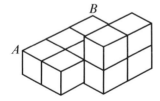

**(2 marks)**

# Translations, reflections and rotations

1  On the grid, plot the points with coordinates (−4, 1), (−2, 1) and (−2, −2).
Label the triangle A.

(a) On the grid, translate A by the vector $\begin{pmatrix} 6 \\ 2 \end{pmatrix}$.
Label the new triangle B.

$\begin{pmatrix} 6 \\ 2 \end{pmatrix}$ means 6 units to the right and 2 units up.

**(2 marks)**

(b) On the grid, reflect A in the line $y = x$ and label the new triangle C.

First, draw in the line $y = x$.

**(2 marks)**

2  On the grid, plot the points with coordinates (3, 5), (3, 2) and (6, 2). Label the triangle D.

(a) On the grid, reflect D in the line $x = 1$.
Label the new triangle E.

First, draw the line $x = 1$.

**(2 marks)**

(b) On the grid, rotate D 90° clockwise about (1, 0) and label the new triangle F.

You can use tracing paper to help you with rotation questions.

**(2 marks)**

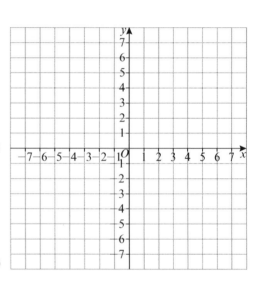

3  On the grid, plot the points with coordinates (2, 0), (1, 3) and (4, 3). Label the triangle G.

**Guided**

(a) Rotate G 180° about the point (−1, −1) and label the new triangle H.

**(2 marks)**

(b) Translate G by $\begin{pmatrix} -4 \\ 2 \end{pmatrix}$ and label the new triangle I.

**(2 marks)**

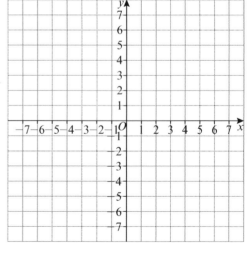

# Enlargement

**1** Join the points on the grid to form a triangle. Label this A.

(a) Enlarge A with a scale factor 2, centre (0, 0).
Label this new triangle B.

**(2 marks)**

(b) Enlarge A with scale factor $\frac{1}{2}$, centre (0, 0).
Label this new triangle C.

> To enlarge through point $(a, b)$, draw lines from $(a, b)$ through vertices and apply the factor.

**(2 marks)**

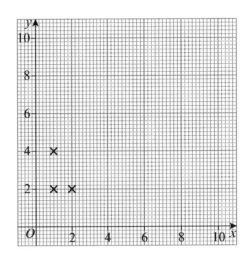

**2** Join the points on the grid to form a triangle. Label this D.

**Guided**

(a) Enlarge D with a scale factor 3, centre (0, 0).
Label this new triangle E.

**(2 marks)**

(b) Enlarge D with a scale factor −1, centre (4, 4).
Label this new triangle F.

**(2 marks)**

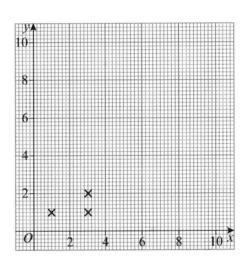

**3** Join the points to form 2 rectangles, G and H. Describe fully the single transformation that maps shape G onto H.

**Guided**

> Give the scale factor, and centre of enlargement.

...............................................................................

...............................................................................

**(3 marks)**

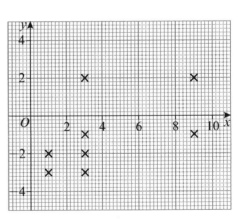

89

# Combining transformations

**1**   (a)   Reflect shape **A** in the *x*-axis.
Label the new shape **B**.

**(2 marks)**

(b)   Translate shape **B** by the vector $\begin{pmatrix} -4 \\ 3 \end{pmatrix}$
Label this new shape **C**.

> Move the shape 4 units to the left and 3 units up.

**(2 marks)**

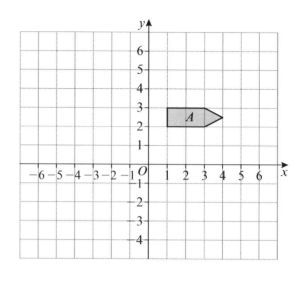

**PROBLEM SOLVED!**

**2**   (a)   Reflect shape **T** in the line $y = x$
Label this new shape **V**.

> Draw the line $y = x$

> You will need to use problem-solving skills throughout your exam – **be prepared!**

**(2 marks)**

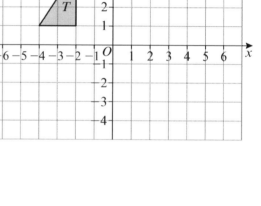

(b)   Rotate shape **V** by 90° about the point (1, 1) anticlockwise. Label this new shape **W**.

> Use tracing paper to rotate this shape.

**(2 marks)**

(c)   What single transformation maps shape **T** onto **W**?

**(2 marks)**

> Rotation, reflection, enlargement or translation?
> You must give details along with the correct transformation.

**PROBLEM SOLVED!**

**3**   (a)   Describe the single transformation that maps shape **A** onto shape **B**.   **(2 marks)**

> You will need to use problem-solving skills throughout your exam – **be prepared!**

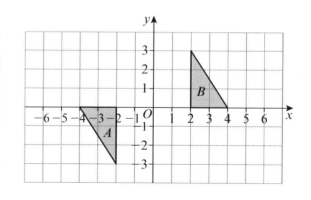

(b)   Reflect shape **B** in the *x*-axis.
Label this shape **C**.   **(2 marks)**

(c)   What single transformation maps shape **A** onto shape **C**?   **(2 marks)**

# Bearings

**1** Measure the following bearings.

(a) *B* from *A*

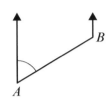

B from A means you start measuring from A.

......... **(2 marks)**

(b) *A* from *B*

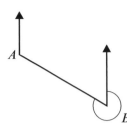

Bearings are always measured from north, clockwise and written in 3 figures.

......... **(2 marks)**

**2** A ship (*S*) sails due west for 10 km to an island (*I*). It then sails for 8 km on a bearing of 110° to a lighthouse *L*. Calculate the bearing of the island from the lighthouse.

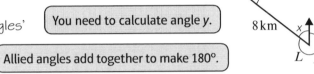

Not drawn to scale.

Angles *x* and 110° are 'allied angles'

You need to calculate angle *y*.

First calculate angle *x*

Allied angles add together to make 180°.

$$x = 180° - 110° = .........°$$

Bearing of *I* from *L* = 360° − *x*

Angles around a point add up to 360°.

$$= 360° - .........°$$

$$= .........°$$

This question can be answered in a few different ways!

**(2 marks)**

**3** Kareem travels 12 km from his home (*A*) due south to his friend's house (*B*). They then travel together on a bearing of 108° for 12 km to the shops (*C*). Calculate the bearing of *C* from *A*.

Not drawn to scale.

First calculate angle *x*

You need to calculate the angle *y*. Notice this is an isosceles triangle.

$$180° - 108° = .........°$$

$$x = .........° ÷ 2 = .........°$$

Isosceles triangles have two equal sides and angles.

Bearing of *C* from *A* = 180° − .........°

$$= .........°$$

Angles on a straight line add to 180°.

**(3 marks)**

**4** *D*, *E* and *F* are 3 sheep in a field. *E* is 2.5 m due east from *D*. *F* is 3.6 m due south from *E*. Calculate the bearing of *F* from *D*. Round your answer to 3 s.f.

ROBLEM SOLVED!

Not drawn to scale.

First calculate angle *x* using trigonometry

Notice this is a right-angled triangle.

$$\tan(x) = \frac{.......}{......} = ........$$

$$x = \tan^{-1}(......) = .........°$$

Bearing of *F* from *D* = 90° + *x*

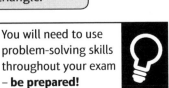

You will need to use problem-solving skills throughout your exam – **be prepared!**

$$= 90° + .........° = .........°$$

$$= .........° \text{ (3 s.f.)}$$

**(4 marks)**

91

# Scale drawings and maps

**1** A replica model car has a scale of 1 : 50.

(a) The length of the model car is 8 cm.
Calculate the actual length of the car.

8 × ......... = ......... cm

**(1 mark)**

(b) The length of the actual car is 375 cm.
Calculate the length of the model car.

375 ÷ ......... = ......... cm

**(1 mark)**

**2** *A* and *B* are towns on a map. The scale is 1 : 200 000
Calculate the distance between the two towns in km.

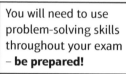 

You will need to use problem-solving skills throughout your exam – **be prepared!**

•
*B*

•
*A*

.........   Remember to convert your final answer to km.   **(3 marks)**

**3** Annalisa wants to spend a day walking in the Lake District. She owns two maps, each using a different scale. Map 1 uses a scale 1 : 600 000 and map 2 uses a scale 1 : 100 000. Which map would be better to use and why?

.................................................................................................................

.................................................................................................................

**(2 marks)**

**4** The diagram shows a wall with windows. Sophia is painting the wall but wants to know how many tins of paint to buy. One tin of paint covers 3 m².

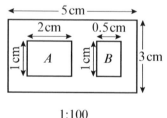

1:100

Total area = 500 × 300 = ......... cm²

Window A = ......... × ......... = ......... cm²

Window B = ......... × ......... = ......... cm²

Area of wall = ......... − (......... + .........)

= ......... cm²

......... cm² ÷ 10 000 = ........ m²

Remember 1 m² = 10 000 cm²

Total tins needed = ......... m² ÷ 3 = ........

= ........ tins

**(5 marks)**

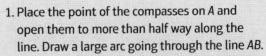

# Constructions 1

1   Use a ruler and compasses to construct the perpendicular bisector of *AB*.

> 1. Place the point of the compasses on *A* and open them to more than half way along the line. Draw a large arc going through the line *AB*.
> 2. Without changing the size of your compasses, do the same at point *B*.
> 3. Draw a line through where the two arcs meet. This line will perpendicularly bisect *AB*.

A ————————————————————— B

> Never erase your construction lines.

**(2 marks)**

2   Use a ruler and compasses to construct a perpendicular line through point *C*.

> 1. Place the point of the compasses on *C* and draw an arc either side, cutting the line (labelled *A* and *B*).
> 2. Now follow the same instructions as question 1, using the points the arcs cut the line as the new end points.

A ——————————— C —————— B

**(3 marks)**

3   Use a ruler and compasses to construct a perpendicular line from point *D* to the line *AB*.

> Guided

× *D*

> Follow the same instructions as question 2 (and so question 1), but from point *D*.

A ————————————————————— B

**(3 marks)**

# Constructions 2

**4** Use a ruler and compasses to bisect the angle *ABC*.

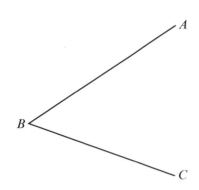

1. Put the point of your compasses at the vertex of the angle (*B*) and draw an arc cutting through the lines *AB* and *BC*.
2. Without changing the size of your compasses, put the point where the arc meets *AB* and draw another arc in-between the points *A* and *C*.
3. Do the same where the arc meets the line *BC*.
4. The new arcs should meet. Draw a line from *B* through where these arcs meet.

Never erase your construction lines.   **(2 marks)**

**5** Use a ruler and compasses to construct a triangle *ABC* with sides 6.5 cm, 5 cm and 4 cm.

1. Draw a 6.5 cm horizontal line *AB*.
2. Open your compasses to 5 cm and place the point at *A*. Draw an arc above the line *AB*.
3. Open your compasses to 4 cm and repeat step 2 at point *B*.
4. Draw straight lines, from where these lines intersect, to *A* and *B*.

*A* ————— 6.5 cm ————— *B*

**(3 marks)**

**6** Use a ruler and compasses to construct a 45° angle.

**PROBLEM SOLVED!**

You will need to bisect a 90° angle.

You will need to use problem-solving skills throughout your exam – **be prepared!**

**(3 marks)**

**7** Use a ruler and compasses to construct a 60° angle.

**PROBLEM SOLVED!**

You will need to construct an equilateral triangle.

You will need to use problem-solving skills throughout your exam – **be prepared!**

**(3 marks)**

# Loci

1   Draw the locus of points equidistant from the points *A* and *B*.

   *A* •

> This is the perpendicular bisector of the line *AB*.

   • *B*                                                                    **(2 marks)**

2   Draw the locus of points 2.5 cm away from the point *C*.

> This is a circle with radius 3 cm and centre *C*.

   •
   *C*

                                                                           **(2 marks)**

3   Draw the locus of points 2.5 cm away from the line *DE*.

> 1. Draw semicircles of radius 2.5 cm at *D* and *E*.
> 2. Connect the semicircles with parallel lines. These should also be 2.5 cm away from the line *DE*.

   *D* ——————————— *E*

                                                                           **(2 marks)**

4   A supermarket is 50 km away from Beth's house and 35 km away from Colin's house. Using the scale 1 cm to 10 km, show the more southerly location where the supermarket could be.

 › Guided

**PROBLEM SOLVED!**

> You will need to use problem-solving skills throughout your exam – **be prepared!**

   N
   ↑

   Beth's House
   ✕

   Colin's House
   ✕                                                                       **(3 marks)**

# Congruent triangles

**1** Prove that the triangles *ABC* and *DEF* are congruent.

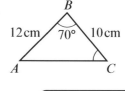

Not drawn to scale.

*AB* = *DF* (both 12 cm)

*BC* = ...... (both 10 cm)

Angle ...... = Angle *DFE* (both 70°)

Hence, triangles *ABC* and *DEF* are congruent.

These triangles are congruent because 2 sides and the included angle are the same (SAS).

The condition that has been satisfied is SAS.    **(3 marks)**

**2** Prove that the triangles *XYZ* and *UVW* are congruent.

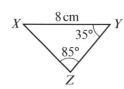

Not drawn to scale.

*XY* = ...... (both 8 cm)

Angle *XZY* = Angle ...... (both 85°)

Angle ...... = Angle ...... (both ......)

Hence, triangles *XYZ* and *UVW* are congruent.

The condition that has been satisfied is ......

These triangles are congruent because 2 angles and a corresponding side are the same (ASA).

Sometimes you might have to calculate a missing angle in the triangle.

**(3 marks)**

**3** The triangle *XYZ* is an isosceles triangle. *WY* is perpendicular to *XZ*.

**PROBLEM SOLVED!**

(a) Prove triangle *WXY* and *WYZ* are congruent.

These triangles are congruent because there is a right angle and the hypotenuse and one other side are the same (RHS).

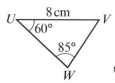

Not drawn to scale.

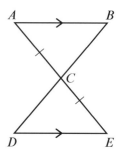

You will need to use problem-solving skills throughout your exam – **be prepared!**

The condition that has been satisfied is ......    **(3 marks)**

(b) Find the area of triangle *XYZ* if *XZ* = 10 cm and *XY* = 13 cm.

......    Use Pythagoras' theorem to find *WY*.    **(3 marks)**

**4** Prove that triangle *ABC* is congruent to *CDE*.

As there are parallel sides here, you can find missing angles by using alternate, corresponding and vertically opposite rules.

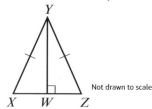

*AC* = ......

Angle *ABC* = Angle *CDE* because they are ...... angles.

Angle ...... = Angle *CED* because they are ...... angles.

Hence, ..............................................................

The condition that has been satisfied is ......    **(3 marks)**

# Similar shapes 1

**1** These two triangles are mathematically similar.

(a) Calculate the length of *YZ*.

Linear scale factor = 15 ÷ 5 = ......

| If two shapes are mathematically similar then each side is enlarged by the same linear scale factor. |

$YZ = 3 \times QR$

$= 3 \times ...... = ......$ cm

**(1 mark)**

(b) Calculate the length of *PQ*.

$XY = 3 \times PQ$

$...... = 3 \times PQ$

$PQ = 36 ÷ ...... = ......$ cm

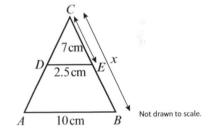

Not drawn to scale.

| • When you are calculating the larger shape's side you must multiply by the scale factor.<br>• When you are calculating the smaller shape's side you must divide by the scale factor. |

**(1 mark)**

**2** Triangle *ABC* is mathematically similar to triangle *CDE*. Calculate the missing side length *x*.

Linear scale factor = ...... ÷ ...... = ......

$BC = 7 \times ...... = ......$ cm

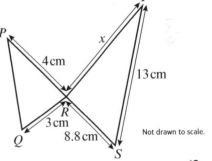

Not drawn to scale.

**(2 marks)**

**3** Triangle *PQR* and *RST* are mathematically similar.

Calculate the length of *RT*.

**Guided**

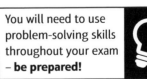

Not drawn to scale.

.........

**(3 marks)**

**PROBLEM SOLVED!**

**4** Triangle *ABC* and *CDE* are mathematically similar. Calculate the missing side length *y*.

| You will need to use problem-solving skills throughout your exam – **be prepared!** |

Linear scale factor = $AC ÷ CD$

$= 66 ÷ ...... = ......$

$DE = 44 ÷ ...... = ......$ cm

| Split up into two separate triangles. |

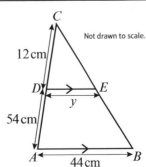

Not drawn to scale.

**(3 marks)**

# Similar shapes 2

**5** These two shapes are mathematically similar.

The smaller star is 6 cm long and the larger star is 9 cm long. Calculate the area of the larger star if the area of the smaller star is 20 cm².

6 cm  20 cm²  9 cm

Not drawn to scale.

Linear scale factor = 9 ÷ ...... = ......

Area scale factor = (linear scale factor)²

Always calculate the linear scale factor first.

= ......² = ......

Area of large star = 20 × ......

= ...... cm²  **(3 marks)**

**6** These two 3D shapes are mathematically similar.

If the volume of *B* is 80 cm³, calculate the volume of *A*. Round your answer to 1 d.p.

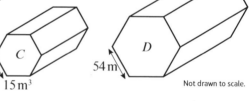

*A*   8 cm   *B*   80 cm³   24 cm

Not drawn to scale.

Linear scale factor = ...... ÷ ...... = ......

Volume scale factor = (linear scale factor)³

= ......³ = ......

Volume of A = 80 ÷ ...... = ...... cm³

= ...... cm³ (1 d.p.)  **(3 marks)**

Guided

**PROBLEM SOLVED!**

**7** *C* and *D* are mathematically similar regular hexagonal prisms. The volume of *C* is 15 m³ and the cross-sectional area of *D* is 600 m².

(a) Calculate the volume of shape *D*. Round your answer to the nearest m³.

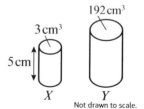

*C*   *D*   4 m   54 m   15 m³

Not drawn to scale.

............ **(3 marks)**

(b) Calculate the cross-sectional area of shape *C*. Round your answer to the nearest m².

............ **(2 marks)**

**PROBLEM SOLVED!**

**8** The two cylinders *X* and *Y* are mathematically similar.

*X* has volume 3 cm³ and *Y* has volume 192 cm³.

(a) Calculate the height of cylinder *Y* if cylinder *X* has height 5 cm.

You will need to use problem-solving skills throughout your exam – **be prepared!**

Volume scale factor = 192 ÷ ...... = ......

Linear scale factor = $\sqrt[3]{\text{(volume scale factor)}}$

= $\sqrt[3]{......}$

= ......

192 cm³   3 cm³   5 cm   *X*   *Y*

Not drawn to scale.

Height of cylinder Y = 5 × ...... = ...... cm  **(3 marks)**

(b) Calculate the cross-sectional area of *X* if the area of *Y* is 80 cm².

............ **(2 marks)**

# The sine rule

**1** Find the length of the missing sides labelled with a letter. Round your answers to 3 s.f.

(a)

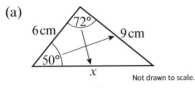

6 cm   72°   9 cm

50°

$x$

Not drawn to scale.

> When finding a missing side it is best to use $\frac{a}{\sin A} = \frac{b}{\sin B} = \frac{c}{\sin C}$
> You must have two pairs of opposite angles and sides, including the length you are calculating.

$$\frac{x}{\sin \dots} = \frac{9}{\sin 50}$$

$$x = \frac{9 \times \sin \dots}{\sin 50}$$

> Rearrange to make $x$ the subject.

$x = \dots$ cm

$x = \dots$ cm (3 s.f.)            **(3 marks)**

(b)

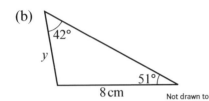

42°

$y$

51°

8 cm        Not drawn to scale.

............        **(3 marks)**

**2** Find the missing angles labelled with a letter. Round your answers to 3 s.f.

(a)

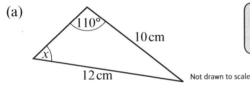

110°   10 cm

$x$

12 cm     Not drawn to scale.

> When finding a missing angle it is best to use
> $\frac{\sin A}{a} = \frac{\sin B}{b} = \frac{\sin C}{c}$

$$\frac{\sin x}{\dots} = \frac{\sin 110}{12}$$

$$\sin x = \frac{10 \times \dots}{12} = \dots$$

$x = \dots °$

> Rearrange to make $\sin x$ the subject.

$x = \sin^{-1}(\dots)$

$x = \dots °$ (3 s.f.)            **(3 marks)**

(b)

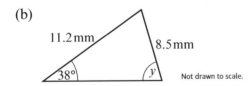

11.2 mm     8.5 mm

38°        $y$     Not drawn to scale.

............        **(3 marks)**

**3** A ship sails from port $A$ to port $B$ on a bearing of 071° for 45 km. It then sails 38 km on a bearing of 164° to port $C$. Finally, it travels 76 km on a bearing of 275° back to port $A$. Calculate the bearing of port $C$ from port $A$. Round your answer to the nearest degree.

> You will need to use problem-solving skills throughout your exam – **be prepared!**

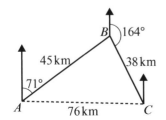

$B$  164°

45 km     38 km

71°

$A$        76 km        $C$     Not drawn to scale.

............        **(4 marks)**

# The cosine rule

**1** Find the lengths of the missing sides labelled with a letter. Round your answers to 3 s.f.

(a)

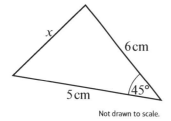

5 cm   6 cm   45°   *x*

Not drawn to scale.

$x^2 = 6^2 + 5^2 - 2 \times \text{......} \times \text{......} \times \cos \text{......}$

$x^2 = \text{......}$

$x = \sqrt{\text{......}}$

$x = \text{......}$

$x = \text{......}$ cm (3 s.f.)

> The cosine rule is $a^2 = b^2 + c^2 - 2bc \cos A$.
>
> The side you are calculating needs to be opposite a given angle.

**(3 marks)**

(b)

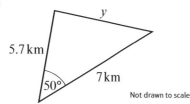

5.7 km   *y*   7 km   50°

Not drawn to scale.

............  **(3 marks)**

**2** Find the missing angles labelled with a letter. Round your answers to 3 s.f.

(a)

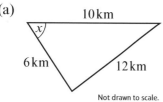

10 km   *x*   6 km   12 km

Not drawn to scale.

$\cos x = \dfrac{10^2 + 6^2 - \text{......}^2}{2 \times \text{......} \times \text{......}}$

$\cos x = \text{......}$

$x = \cos^{-1}(\text{......})$

$x = \text{......}°$

$x = \text{......}°$ (3 s.f.)

> When finding a missing angle you will need to rearrange the formula to get $\cos A = \dfrac{b^2 + c^2 - a^2}{2bc}$

**(3 marks)**

(b)

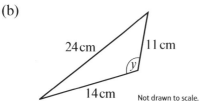

24 cm   11 cm   *y*   14 cm

Not drawn to scale.

............  **(3 marks)**

**3** Calculate the size of the largest angle. Round your answer to the nearest degree.

**PROBLEM SOLVED!**

> You will need to use problem-solving skills throughout your exam – **be prepared!**

> The largest angle is always opposite the longest side.

6.5 cm   7.7 cm   8.2 cm

Not drawn to scale.

............  **(3 marks)**

**4** Mandeep is looking at a house from his garden. The angle of elevation from where he is standing to the edge of the roof is 35°. Calculate the height of the wall, labelled *x*. Round your answers to 1 d.p.

**Guided**

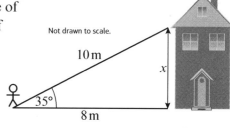

Not drawn to scale.

10 m   *x*   35°   8 m

............  **(3 marks)**

# Triangles and segments

1   Calculate the area of these triangles, rounding your final answer to 3 s.f.

(a)

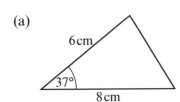

> The area formula for a triangle where you are not given the perpendicular height is $A = \frac{1}{2}ab\sin C$.
>
> $a$ and $b$ are two sides with an angle $C$ in-between them.

$$\text{Area} = \frac{1}{2} \times 6 \times \ldots\ldots \times \sin\ldots\ldots$$

$$= \ldots\ldots \; cm^2$$

$$= \ldots\ldots \; cm^2 \; (3 \; s.f.)$$

**(2 marks)**

(b)

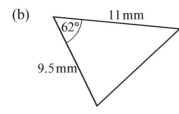

.............. **(2 marks)**

2   Calculate the area of the shaded region. Round your final answer to 1 d.p.

> Area of sector $= \pi r^2 \times \frac{\theta}{360°}$ The radius of the circle is 7 cm.

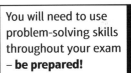

> You will need to use problem-solving skills throughout your exam – **be prepared!**

(a)

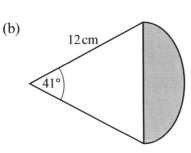

$$\text{Area of sector} = \pi \times \ldots\ldots^2 \times \frac{\ldots\ldots}{360}$$

$$= \ldots\ldots \; cm^2$$

$$\text{Area of triangle} = \frac{1}{2} \times \ldots\ldots \times \ldots\ldots \times \sin\ldots\ldots = \ldots\ldots \; cm^2$$

Area of shaded section = Area of sector – Area of triangle

$$= \ldots\ldots - \ldots\ldots = \ldots\ldots \; cm^2$$

$$= \ldots\ldots \; cm^2 \; (1 \; d.p.)$$

**(4 marks)**

(b)

.............. **(4 marks)**

3   Calculate the area of this triangle, rounding your final answer to the nearest $m^2$.

First, calculate $x$ using the sine rule

$$\frac{\sin x}{5.1} = \frac{\sin \cdots}{8.6}$$

$$\sin x = \frac{5.1 \times \sin \cdots}{8.6} = \ldots\ldots$$

$$x = \sin^{-1}(\ldots\ldots) = \ldots\ldots°$$

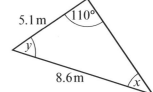

There are 180° in a triangle so $y = 180° - (110° + \ldots\ldots°) = \ldots\ldots°$

$$\text{Area of triangle} = \frac{1}{2} \times 5.1 \times \ldots\ldots \times \sin\ldots\ldots$$

$$= \ldots\ldots \; m^2$$

$$= \ldots\ldots \; m^2 \; (\text{nearest whole number})$$

> Notice the given angle is not between the two sides.

**(4 marks)**

# Pythagoras in 3D

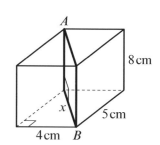

**1** A cuboid has dimensions 4 cm by 5 cm by 8 cm. Calculate the length of $AB$, rounding your final answer to 3 s.f.

First calculate the length of $x$ using Pythagoras' theorem.

$x^2 = 4^2 + \ldots\ldots^2 = \ldots\ldots$

$x = \sqrt{\ldots\ldots}$   $x = \ldots\ldots$ cm

> Look out for all of the right-angled triangles in this cuboid.

Now use Pythagoras' theorem again to calculate $AB$.

$AB^2 = \ldots\ldots^2 + 8^2 = \ldots\ldots$

$AB = \sqrt{\ldots\ldots} = \ldots\ldots$ cm

$AB = \ldots\ldots$ cm (3 s.f.)   **(4 marks)**

**2** Calculate the perpendicular height $PQ$ of this pyramid. Round your answer to 3 s.f.

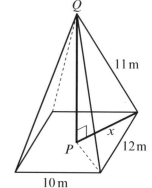

First, use Pythagoras' theorem to calculate the length of $x$.

Diagonal length $= \sqrt{10^2 + \ldots\ldots^2}$

> You will need to calculate the diagonal of the base first and then halve it.

$= \ldots\ldots$ m

$x = \ldots\ldots \div 2 = \ldots\ldots$ m

Now use Pythagoras' theorem to calculate the perpendicular height.

$11^2 = PQ^2 + \ldots\ldots^2$

$PQ^2 = 11^2 - \ldots\ldots^2$

$PQ = \ldots\ldots = \sqrt{\ldots\ldots} = \ldots\ldots$ m

$= \ldots\ldots$ m (3 s.f.)   **(4 marks)**

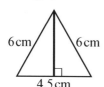
**PROBLEM SOLVED!**

**3** (a) An isosceles triangle has sides 6 cm, 6 cm and 4.5 cm.

Calculate the perpendicular height of this triangle, rounding your final answer to 1 d.p.

> You will need to use problem-solving skills throughout your exam – **be prepared!**

6 cm  6 cm

4.5 cm

............   **(2 marks)**

(b) The isosceles triangle forms the end faces of the triangular prism shown with a length of 4.5 cm. Calculate the length of $xy$, rounding your answer to 3 s.f.

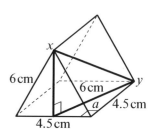

> Calculate length $a$ first and then use your answer to part (a) to calculate $xy$.

............   **(4 marks)**

# Trigonometry in 3D

**1** (a) Calculate the length of the diagonal *AD*, rounding your answer to 1 d.p.

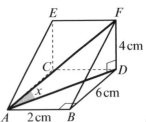

$AD^2 = 2^2 + \ldots\ldots^2 = \ldots\ldots$

$AD = \sqrt{\ldots\ldots} = \ldots\ldots$ cm

$AD = \ldots\ldots$ cm (1 d.p.)

**(2 marks)**

(b) Calculate the angle between the line *AF* and the base *ABCD*, labelled *x* on the diagram. Round your final answer to 1 d.p.

$\tan x = \dfrac{\text{opp}}{\text{hyp}} = \ldots\ldots$

$x = \tan^{-1}(\ldots\ldots) = \ldots\ldots°$

$x = \ldots\ldots°$ (1 d.p.)

> You need to use trigonometry here and your answer to part (a).

**(3 marks)**

**2** Calculate the angle between the line *BF* and the base *ABCD*, labelled *y* on the diagram. Round your final answer to 3 s.f.

Guided

PROBLEM SOLVED!

> You will need to use problem-solving skills throughout your exam – **be prepared!**

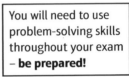

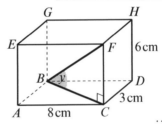

$\ldots\ldots$    **(5 marks)**

**3** This pyramid has a rectangular base, dimensions 3.2 km by 8.7 km and a perpendicular height of 7.5 km.

PROBLEM SOLVED!

> You will need to use problem-solving skills throughout your exam – **be prepared!**

(a) Find the length *AE*, rounding your answer to 3 s.f.

First, use Pythagoras' theorem to calculate the length of *x*.

Diagonal length $= \sqrt{3.2^2 + \ldots\ldots^2}$

> You will need to calculate the diagonal *AC* and then halve it.

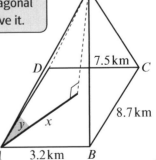

$= \ldots\ldots$

$x = \ldots\ldots \div 2 = \ldots\ldots$ cm

Now use Pythagoras' theorem to find the length of *AE*.

$AE^2 = \ldots\ldots^2 + 7.5^2 = \ldots\ldots$

$AE = \sqrt{\ldots\ldots} = \ldots\ldots$ km

$AE = \ldots\ldots$ km (3 s.f.)

**(4 marks)**

(b) Calculate the angle between the line *AE* and the base *ABCD*, labelled *y* on the diagram. Round your final answer to 3 s.f.

$\tan y = \dfrac{7.5}{\ldots\ldots} = \ldots\ldots$

$y = \tan^{-1}(\ldots\ldots) = \ldots\ldots°$

$y = \ldots\ldots°$ (3 s.f.)

> As you now know all 3 lengths of the right-angled triangle you can use either sin, cos or tan.

**(2 marks)**

103

# Circle facts

 **1** *B* and *C* are points on the circumference of a circle, centre *O*.

*AB* and *AC* are tangents to the circle.

Angle *OAC* is 32°.

Calculate angle *AOC*, giving reasons for your answers.

Angle *ACO* = ......° because the angle between a tangent and the radius is ......°

Angle *AOC* = 180° − (32° + ......°) = ......° because angles in a triangle

         add up to ......°                    **(2 marks)**

 **2** *X* and *Z* are points on the circumference of a circle, centre *O*.

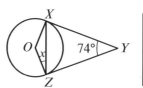

*YX* and *YZ* are tangents to the circle and *XZ* is a chord.

Angle *XYZ* is 74°.

Calculate angle *OZX*, giving reasons for your answers.

> You will need to use problem-solving skills throughout your exam – **be prepared!**

**PROBLEM SOLVED!**

> Triangles *XYZ* and *XOZ* are both isosceles triangles.

Angle *OXY* and *OZY* = ......° because .........................................................

................................................................................................................

Angle *XOZ* = 360° − (74° + ......° + ......°) = ......° because angles in a quadrilateral add up to ......°

Triangle *XOZ* is an isosceles triangle because the two radii are the same length so angle *OXZ* = angle *OZX*.

180° − ......° = ......° because angles in a triangle add up to ......°

*x* = ......° ÷ 2 = ......°                       **(4 marks)**

 **3** *B* and *C* are points on the circumference of a circle, centre *O*.

**Guided**

**PROBLEM SOLVED!**

*AB* and *AC* are tangents to the circle.

Prove that the triangles *ABO* and *ACO* are congruent.

> You will need to use problem-solving skills throughout your exam – **be prepared!**

                                              **(3 marks)**

# Circle theorems

**1** *A*, *B* and *C* are points on the circumference of a circle, centre *O*.
Angle *AOC* = 76°

(a) Find the size of angle *ABC*

Angle ABC = 76° ÷ ......° = ......°

(b) Give a reason for your answer

The angle at the centre is t...... the angle at the circumference.    **(3 marks)**

**2** *A*, *B*, *C* and *D* are points on the circumference of a circle, centre *O*. Angle *ABO* = 31°.
Find the size of angle *DCO*. Give reasons for your answer.

Angle DCO = ......°

because angles in the same segment on a circle are e......    **(2 marks)**

**3** *A*, *B*, *C* and *D* are points on the circumference of a circle, centre *O*.

Angle *BOD* = 162° and *ABCD* is a cyclic quadrilateral. Find the size of angle *BAD*, giving reasons for your answers.

| You will need to use problem-solving skills throughout your exam – **be prepared!** |

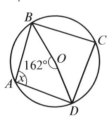

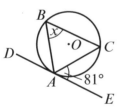

............    **(3 marks)**

**4** *A*, *B* and *C* are points on the circumference of a circle, centre *O*.

*DE* is a tangent to the circle going through point *A*.
Angle *CAE* = 81°

(a) Find the size of angle *ABC*.

Angle ABC = ......°

(b) Give a reason for your answer.

This is a special theorem called the a ...... s ...... theorem. The angle between a chord and a tangent is e...... to the angle in the a......

s......    **(2 marks)**

105

# Vectors

**1** Write each of the vectors **c** to **f** in terms of **a** and/or **b**.

> Vectors can be written in bold but you will have to underline them.

$c = \ldots\ldots \mathbf{a}$

> When you are going in the opposite direction to the arrow, the vector is negative.

$d = - \ldots\ldots \mathbf{b}$

$e = \mathbf{a} + \ldots\ldots \mathbf{b}$

$f = \ldots\ldots \mathbf{a} - \ldots\ldots \mathbf{b}$          **(4 marks)**

**2** $ABCD$ is a parallelogram.

$AB$ is parallel to $CD$.

$AD$ is parallel to $BC$.

Write down the following vectors in terms of **a** and/or **b**:

(a) $\overrightarrow{DB} = \overrightarrow{DA} + \overrightarrow{AB} = \mathbf{b} + \ldots\ldots$

(b) $\overrightarrow{CD} = \ldots\ldots$

(c) $\overrightarrow{BD} = \overrightarrow{BA} + \longrightarrow AD = (\ldots\ldots + \ldots\ldots)$

(d) $\overrightarrow{CA} = \ldots\ldots + \ldots\ldots = - \ldots\ldots + \ldots\ldots$ or $\ldots\ldots - \ldots\ldots$          **(4 marks)**

**3** $ABC$ is a triangle.

$M$ is the midpoint of $AC$.

Write down the following vectors in terms of **p** and/or **q**:

(a) $\overrightarrow{BC} = \overrightarrow{BA} + \overrightarrow{AC} = -\ldots\mathbf{q} + \ldots\mathbf{p}$ or $\ldots\mathbf{p} - \ldots\mathbf{q}$

(b) $\overrightarrow{AM} = \ldots\ldots$

(c) $\overrightarrow{BM} = \overrightarrow{BA} + \overrightarrow{AM} = - \ldots\mathbf{q} + \ldots\mathbf{p}$ or $\ldots\mathbf{p} - \ldots\mathbf{q}$          **(3 marks)**

> Guided

> **PROBLEM SOLVED!**

**4** Write down the following vectors in terms of **a** and/or **b**. Give your answer in its simplest form.

> You will need to use problem-solving skills throughout your exam – **be prepared!**

(a) $\overrightarrow{CA} =$

............ **(2 marks)**

(b) $\overrightarrow{AD} =$

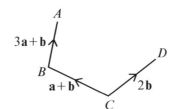

............ **(2 marks)**

# Vector proof

**1** *ABCD* is a rectangle.

*P*, *Q*, *R* and *S* are the midpoints of each of the sides.

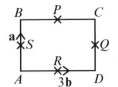

(a) Find the following vectors in terms of **a** and/or **b**.

(i) $\overrightarrow{BC} = \ldots$ **b**

(ii) $\overrightarrow{DB} = \overrightarrow{DA} + \overrightarrow{AB} = -\ldots$ **b** $+ \ldots$ **a** or $\ldots$ **a** $- \ldots$ **b**

(iii) $\overrightarrow{BP} = \ldots$

(iv) $\overrightarrow{AP} = \overrightarrow{AB} + \overrightarrow{BP} = \ldots$ **a** $+ \ldots$ **b**    **(4 marks)**

(b) Show that *PQ* is parallel to *RS*.

$\overrightarrow{PQ} = \frac{3}{2}$ **b** $- \ldots$ **a**

$\overrightarrow{RS} = -\frac{3}{2}$ **b** $+ \ldots$ **a**

$\overrightarrow{PQ} = -\ldots$ therefore parallel    **(2 marks)**

> Vectors are parallel to each other if they are multiples of each other.

**2** *ABC* is a triangle.

$\overrightarrow{AB} = 6$**a** and $\overrightarrow{AC} = 5$**b**

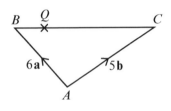

(a) Find $\overrightarrow{BC}$ in terms of **a** and/or **b**.

$\ldots\ldots\ldots$    **(1 mark)**

(b) *Q* is the point on *BC* such that *BQ* : *QC* = 1 : 3

Prove $\overrightarrow{AQ} = \frac{1}{2}(9\mathbf{a} + \frac{5}{2}\mathbf{b})$

$\overrightarrow{BC} = \ldots\ldots\ldots$

$\overrightarrow{BQ} = \frac{1}{4}(\overrightarrow{BC}) = \frac{1}{4}(\ldots\ldots\ldots) = \ldots\ldots\ldots = \ldots\ldots\ldots$

$\overrightarrow{AQ} = \ldots\ldots\ldots = \ldots\ldots\ldots = \frac{1}{2}(\ldots\ldots\ldots)$    **(4 marks)**

**3** *ABC* is a triangle.

*M* is the midpoint of *AB*.

> Guided

> PROBLEM SOLVED!

*P* is the midpoint of *BC*.

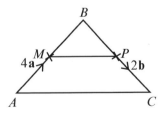

(a) Find the vector $\overrightarrow{AC}$ in terms of **a** and/or **b**.

> You will need to use problem-solving skills throughout your exam – **be prepared!**

$\ldots\ldots\ldots$    **(1 mark)**

(b) Show that *AC* is parallel to *MP*.

**(3 marks)**

# Problem-solving practice 1

**1** Find $x$ if the regular polygon has 20 sides.

Sum of interior angles = ( ...... − 2) × 180° = ......°

So each interior angle = ...... ÷ ...... = ......°

Angles in a Δ add up to 180° so $x = \dfrac{180 - ......}{......} = ......$°

**(4 marks)**

**2** Find the distance between the points $A$ (2, 5) and $B$ (6, 10).

First draw a sketch of the points, and form a right-angled Δ.

Use Pythagoras' theorem to find the length $AB$.

$AB^2 = ......^2 + ......^2$          $AB = ......$ units          **(3 marks)**

**PROBLEM SOLVED!**

**3** The volume of a new style tent formed by a hemisphere and a cylinder is $\dfrac{40}{3}\pi\,\text{m}^3$. The height of the cylinder is equal to the radius of the hemisphere. Find the radius.

You will need to use problem-solving skills throughout your exam – **be prepared!**

Total volume = volume of hemisphere + volume of cylinder

$\dfrac{40}{3}\pi = \dfrac{1}{2} \times \dfrac{4}{3} ...... r^3 + \pi r^2 \times ......$

$\div\,\pi$

$r^3 = ......$

Simplify.

So $r = ......$ m

**(6 marks)**

**Gu̶i̶ded**

**PROBLEM SOLVED!**

**4** A fish tank is filled using a conical water jug.

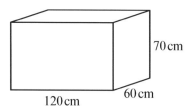

120 cm   60 cm   70 cm

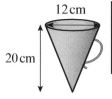

12 cm   20 cm

You will need to use problem-solving skills throughout your exam – **be prepared!**

How many times will the jug need to be filled and emptied into the tank to completely fill the tank?

..............   **(4 marks)**

# Problem-solving practice 2

**5** $ABC$ is a triangle.

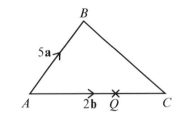

$\overrightarrow{AB} = 5\mathbf{a}$

$\overrightarrow{AC} = 2\mathbf{b}$

(a) Find $\overrightarrow{BC}$.

.............. **(2 marks)**

(b) $Q$ is the point on $AC$ such that $AQ : QC = 2 : 1$.

Prove $\overrightarrow{BQ} = \frac{4}{3}\mathbf{b} - 5\mathbf{a}$

**(3 marks)**

**6** $B$, $D$, $E$ are points on the circumference of a circle, centre $O$.
$BE$ is the diameter of the circle and $AC$ is a tangent to the circle through point $B$.
Angle $ABD = 85°$.
Calculate all of the missing angles in the triangle $BDE$, giving reasons for your answers.

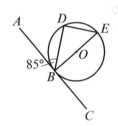

**(6 marks)**

**7** $OBC$ is a sector of a circle, centre $O$.
Show the area of the shaded region can be expressed as $\frac{1}{4}x^2\left(\frac{1}{3}\pi - 1\right)$.

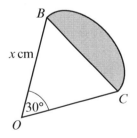

**(4 marks)**

# Mean, median and mode

**1** Find the mean (to 1 d.p.), median and mode of the following numbers.

7   9   1̶   8   7   2   3̶   5   7   8   2̶

> First put the numbers in order.

1  2  2  2  3  5  7  7  2̶  8  9

Mean = $\frac{54}{11}$

> The mean = $\frac{\text{sum of the numbers}}{\text{how many numbers there are}}$

= 4.9

Median = 5

> The median is the middle number.

Mode = 2

> The mode is the most common number.

**(4 marks)**

**2** Find the mean, median and mode of the following ages.

2   7   11   3   3   5

2  3  3  5  7  11

> Put the ages in order.

Mean = $\frac{31}{6}$ = 5.16

**(2 marks)**

Median = $\frac{6̶3 + 1̶1̶}{2}$ = 4̶

> If there are 2 middle numbers, add them together and ÷ 2.

**(1 mark)**

Mode = 3

**(1 mark)**

**3** On sports' day, the times for the 100 m sprint were recorded in seconds:

12.3  13.2  11.9  15.6  12.3  12.7  13.4

For these times, find

(a) the mean

............... **(2 marks)**

(b) the median

............... **(1 mark)**

(c) the mode

............... **(1 mark)**

**4** The mean of five numbers is 20. The mean of three numbers is 24. What is the mean of the other two numbers?

> You will need to use problem-solving skills throughout your exam – **be prepared!**

............ **(3 marks)**

# Frequency table averages

1  The table shows information about the number of siblings a group of children have:

| No. of siblings | Frequency | No. of siblings × frequency |
|---|---|---|
| 0 | 7 | 0 × 7 = ...... |
| 1 | 15 | 1 × 15 = ...... |
| 2 | 5 | 2 × ...... = ...... |
| 3 | 3 | ...... × ...... = ...... |
| 4 | 1 | ...... × ...... = ...... |
| Total frequency. → | ...... | ...... ← Find total number of siblings. |

(a)  Find the mode.

.........   [ The mode is the no. of siblings with highest frequency. ]   **(1 mark)**

(b)  Find the median.

$$\text{Median} = \frac{...... + 1}{2}\text{th value}$$   [ The median is the $\frac{\text{total frequency} + 1}{2}$ th value. ]

$$= ......\text{th value} = ......$$   **(2 marks)**

(c)  Find the mean to 1 decimal place.

$$\text{Mean} = \frac{\text{total no. of siblings}}{\text{total frequency}} = \frac{......}{......} = ......$$   **(3 marks)**

2  The table shows information about the number of texts received in a week by a group of pupils.

| No. of texts, $t$ | Frequency | Midpoint | Midpoint × Frequency | |
|---|---|---|---|---|
| $0 < t \leqslant 10$ | 3 | 5 | 5 × 3 = ...... | For grouped frequency tables, the midpoint will be needed to estimate the mean. |
| $10 < t \leqslant 20$ | 13 | 15 | 15 × 13 = ...... | |
| $20 < t \leqslant 30$ | 15 | ...... | ...... × 15 = ...... | |
| $30 < t \leqslant 40$ | 11 | ...... | ...... × ...... = ...... | |
| $40 < t \leqslant 50$ | 7 | ...... | ...... × ...... = ...... | |
| Total frequency. → | ...... | | ...... ← Total no. of texts. | |

(a)  Write down the modal class.

............   **(1 mark)**

(b)  Write down the class interval that contains the median.

............   **(1 mark)**

(c)  Work out an estimate for the mean number of texts.

$$\text{Mean} = \frac{\text{Total no. of texts}}{\text{Total frequency}} = \frac{......}{......} = ....$$   **(3 marks)**

(d)  What is the probability that a child picked at random received over 30 texts?

[ You will need to use problem-solving skills throughout your exam – **be prepared!** ]

............   **(2 marks)**

# Interquartile range

1  The following is a list of numbers.

3    1    7    19    30    12    5    8    11    2    9

Find

(a)  the median

> Put the numbers in order.

......    2    ......    ......    ......    ......    ......    ......    12    ......    ......

Median = ......th value

> The median is the $\frac{11+1}{2}$th value.

Median = ........................

**(1 mark)**

(b)  the lower and upper quartiles

Lower quartile = ..............rd value

> The lower quartile is the $\frac{11+1}{4}$th value.

Lower quartile = ........................

Upper quartile = ..............th value

> The upper quartile is the $\frac{3(11+1)}{4}$th value.

Upper quartile = ........................

**(4 marks)**

(c)  the interquartile range.

> The interquartile range = upper quartile − lower quartile

Interquartile range = ........................ − ........................

Interquartile range = ........................

**(2 marks)**

2  The table shows information about the number of pets owned by a group of children.

| No. of pets | Frequency |
|:---:|:---:|
| 0 | 3 |
| 1 | 10 |
| 2 | 11 |
| 3 | 5 |
| 4 | 2 |

> Total frequency, $n$, = ......

(a)  Find the interquartile range.

> Lower quartile = $\frac{n+1}{4}$ th value

= ......th value = ......

> Upper quartile = $3\frac{(n+1)}{4}$ th value

= ......th value = ......

So interquartile range = ...... − ...... = ......

**(3 marks)**

(b)  When might it be preferable to use the interquartile range rather than the range as a measure of the spread of the data?

> You will need to use problem-solving skills throughout your exam – **be prepared!**

..................................................................................................    **(1 mark)**

# Line graphs

**1** The table shows a pupil's test results in mathematics over a period of 10 weeks.

| Week | 1 | 2 | 3 | 4 | 5 | 6 | 7 | 8 | 9 | 10 |
|------|---|---|---|---|---|---|---|---|---|----|
| Percentage | 42 | 47 | 52 | 50 | 50 | 55 | 60 | 68 | 70 | 71 |

(a) Draw a line graph to display this data.

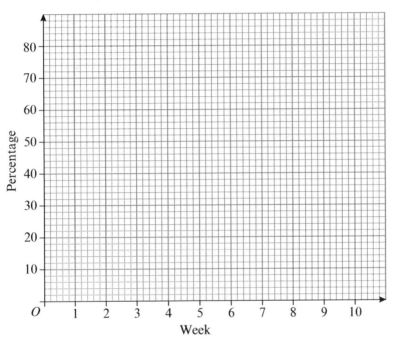

> Plot the points and join them with straight lines.

**(2 marks)**

(b) Between which weeks is the greatest improvement made?

> Greatest improvement = steepest slope.

............ **(1 mark)**

(c) Between which weeks is there a decrease in the percentage?

> Decrease means slope goes down.

............ **(1 mark)**

(d) Write down the range for these results.

> Range = highest value – lowest value.

............ **(1 mark)**

(e) Draw a trend line onto your graph.

> A trend line is a straight line drawn from week 1 to week 10 to show the general pattern of change.

**(1 mark)**

 **PROBLEM SOLVED!**

(f) Could this trend line be used to predict a percentage in week 30? Explain your answer.

> You will need to use problem-solving skills throughout your exam – **be prepared!**

......, because ...........................................

....................................................

.................................................................... **(2 marks)**

# Scatter graphs

**1** Some students measured the lengths of their hands and their feet to the nearest cm, and the results are shown in the table below.

| Length of hand (cm) | 12 | 15 | 13 | 12 | 11 | 12 | 13 | 10 | 11 | 14 |
|---|---|---|---|---|---|---|---|---|---|---|
| Length of foot (cm) | 22 | 24 | 22 | 21 | 20 | 19 | 21 | 18 | 18 | 22 |

Positive correlation reminder.

(a) Draw a scatter graph of the results on the grid. **(2 marks)**

> Do not join the points of a scatter graph.

(b) Describe the correlation.

................. correlation **(1 mark)**

(c) Draw a line of best fit on the graph.

**(1 mark)**

(d) Use your line to estimate the length of the hand of a student whose foot is 23 cm.

............ **(1 mark)**

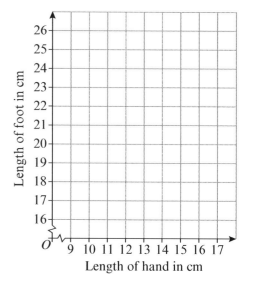

**2** The table shows the exam results of a group of pupils in music and computer science.

| Music | 23 | 78 | 57 | 90 | 38 | 62 | 45 | 11 | 71 |
|---|---|---|---|---|---|---|---|---|---|
| Computer science | 70 | 32 | 53 | 20 | 67 | 49 | 55 | 14 | 41 |

Negative correlation reminder.

(a) Draw a scatter graph of the exam results. **(1 mark)**

(b) What type of correlation does the graph show?

............ correlation **(1 mark)**

(c) A pupil missed the music exam, but got 60% in computer science. Use your graph to estimate what he might have got in music.

> Draw the line of best fit on your graph to estimate.

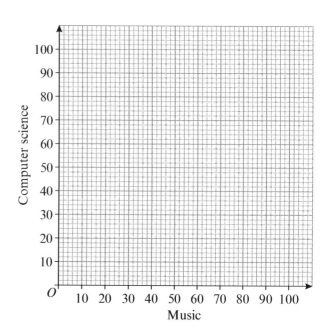

............ **(1 mark)**

# Sampling

**1** (a) Give two advantages of using a sample rather than a census.

..............................................................................

..............................................................................

> A census includes every member of the population. A sample is a smaller group of the population.

**(2 marks)**

(b) Give two advantages of using a census rather than a sample.

..............................................................................

..............................................................................

**(2 marks)**

**2** Which of these are continuous data and which are discrete data?

(a) Height is ................. data.

(b) Shoe sizes are ................. data.

(c) Length of feet is ................. data.

(d) Number of pets is ................. data.

> Discrete data can only take particular values on a numerical scale.

**(4 marks)**

**3** Which of these are qualitative data and which are quantitative data?

(a) Colour of hair is ................. data.

(b) Number of hairs on head is ................. data.

(c) Thickness of a hair is ................. data.

(d) Make of mobile phone is ................. data.

> Quantitative data are numerical observations or measurements.

**(4 marks)**

**4** A supermarket wants to collect information about its shoppers. A survey is taken at 11 am each Monday and Wednesday morning for 3 weeks. Give two ways of improving this survey.

> You will need to use problem-solving skills throughout your exam – **be prepared!**

..............................................................................

..............................................................................

**(2 marks)**

**5** A question in a school survey was 'You stop using your mobile phone by 9 pm every evening, don't you?' Billy said this question was biased. Explain what Billy means, and write an improved question.

> You will need to use problem-solving skills throughout your exam – **be prepared!**

..............................................................................

..............................................................................

> Tick boxes are good in a closed question.

..............................................................................

..............................................................................

**(3 marks)**

# Stratified sampling

**1** The table shows the number of boys and girls in the junior forms at Bowood School.

|  | Year 9 | Year 10 | Year 11 |
|---|---|---|---|
| **Boys** | 42 | 44 | 53 |
| **Girls** | 37 | 45 | 48 |

> The size of each group in a stratified sample is proportional to the size of each group in the population.

The team of inspectors want a stratified sample of 50 pupils according to year group and gender.

(a) How many boys will be in the sample?

No. of boys = ...... + 44 + ...... = 139

Total no. of pupils = 139 + ...... + ...... + ...... = ......

Number of boys in sample = $\frac{......}{......}$ × 50 = ......

> Round to nearest whole number.

**(2 marks)**

(b) How many girls from year 11 will be in the sample?

Year 11 girls = $\frac{......}{269}$ × 50 = ......

**(2 marks)**

**PROBLEM SOLVED!**

**2** A mobile phone company wants to survey its customers using a stratified sample of 500 according to age. The table shows the numbers used in the sample.

| Age, $a$ years | $a < 20$ | $20 \leqslant a < 40$ | $40 \leqslant a < 60$ | $a \geqslant 60$ |
|---|---|---|---|---|
| **Frequency** | 185 | 244 | 50 | 21 |

> You will need to use problem-solving skills throughout your exam – **be prepared!**

The company has 2.1 million customers. Work out an estimate for the number of customers in the under 20 age group.

Fraction of sample under 20 years = $\frac{......}{......}$

So number of customers = $\frac{......}{......}$ × ...... million = ......

**(3 marks)**

Gu~~X~~ed

**3** 120 750 people live in Dean Town. A mobile phone company carried out a survey. It used a random sample of 800 people. 480 of this sample were female. Work out an estimate for the number of males living in Dean Town.

............ **(3 marks)**

# Capture–recapture

1  A zoology student is doing some research into snail populations. 50 snails were captured, marked and released. Later, 150 snails were captured. 15 of these snails were found to be marked.

> Remember   $\dfrac{\text{tagged}}{\text{captured}} = \dfrac{\text{recaptured}}{\text{population}}$

(a) Estimate the size of the snail population, *p*.

The proportion of marked snails = $\dfrac{15}{150} = \dfrac{50}{P}$

> Rearrange to find *p*.

$p = \dfrac{50 \times ......}{......} = ......$   **(2 marks)**

(b) Write down one assumption that you have made.

................................................................................................ **(1 mark)**

2  During a Spring watch project, 180 trout were captured, marked and returned to the river. Later that week, 120 trout were captured and 48 of them were found to be marked.
Find an estimate for the trout population in the river.

Proportion of marked trout = $\dfrac{......}{......} = \dfrac{......}{x}$

Population, $x = \dfrac{...... \times ......}{......} = ......$   **(2 marks)**

3  In a forest, 45 wild boar were captured, tagged and returned to the forest. Later, 35 boar were captured and 15 were found to be tagged. Find an estimate for the population of wild boar in the forest.

............ **(2 marks)**

4  In Florida, the number of alligators was being researched. 320 alligators were captured and tagged. A few weeks later, 240 alligators were captured and 12 of these were already tagged. Estimate the population of alligators in Florida.

............ **(2 marks)**

5  Paul wants to estimate how many frogs are in his pond. He captured 10, marked them and released them back to the pond. Later, 25 frogs are captured and five are found to be marked. Estimate the number of frogs in Paul's pond.

............ **(2 marks)**

# Cumulative frequency

1   In a biology experiment, the heights of 80 plants were measured in cm. The results are shown in the table.

| Height, $h$ in cm | Frequency |
|---|---|
| $0 < h \leqslant 10$ | 2 |
| $10 < h \leqslant 20$ | 8 |
| $20 < h \leqslant 30$ | 18 |
| $30 < h \leqslant 40$ | 20 |
| $40 < h \leqslant 50$ | 18 |
| $50 < h \leqslant 60$ | 14 |

| Height, $h$ in cm | Cumulative frequency |
|---|---|
| $0 < h \leqslant 10$ | 2 |
| $0 < h \leqslant 20$ | 2 + 8 = ...... |
| $0 < h \leqslant 30$ | ...... + 18 = ...... |
| $0 < h \leqslant 40$ | ...... + 20 = ...... |
| $0 < h \leqslant 50$ | ...... + ...... = ...... |
| $0 < h \leqslant 60$ | ...... + ...... = ...... |

Cumulative frequency is a 'running total'.

(a)  Complete the cumulative frequency table for this information.

**(1 mark)**

(b)  On the grid, draw a cumulative frequency graph.

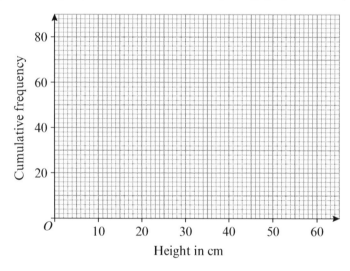

Height in cm

**(2 marks)**

(c)  Use your graph to find an estimate for the median height.

To estimate median, find total frequency ÷ 2 = .........
Read across from this value to the graph and then down.

............   **(2 marks)**

(d)  Use your graph to find an estimate for the interquartile range.

...... − ...... = ......

Interquartile range = upper quartile − lower quartile

**(2 marks)**

(e)  Use your graph to find an estimate for the number of plants that are taller than 45 cm.

............   **(2 marks)**

# Box plots

**1** The box plot shows how long, in minutes, people are waiting for a train.

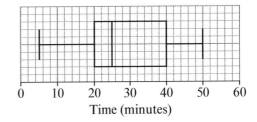

(a) Calculate the median time waited.

Median = ...... minutes

> The median is represented by the middle line inside the 'box'.

**(1 mark)**

(b) Calculate the interquartile range of the time waited.

IQR = UQ − LQ

    = 40 − ......

    = ......

> Interquartile range = upper quartile – lower quartile.
> The lower and upper quartiles are represented by the beginning and end lines of the 'box'.
> It calculates the spread of the middle 50% of the data.

**(2 marks)**

(c) What percentage of people waited 40 minutes or less for a train?

Percentage of people waiting 40 minutes or less = ......%

**(1 mark)**

**2** Pupils in a PE class threw a javelin and their distances, in metres, were recorded.
Using the table of information below, draw a box plot illustrating the javelin distances.

| Lowest distance | 3 m |
|---|---|
| Highest distance | 22 m |
| Median | 14 m |
| Lower quartile | 10 m |
| Upper quartile | 18 m |

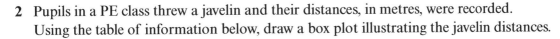

Distance (metres)

**(3 marks)**

**3** The box plot shows the heights, in cm, of a group of people.

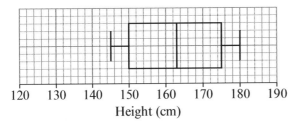

120  130  140  150  160  170  180  190
Height (cm)

(a) Calculate the range of the heights.

Range = ...... − 145 = ...... cm

> Range = highest value – lowest value.

**(1 mark)**

(b) 80 people were asked their heights.
How many people were 150 cm or less?

25% of 80 = 80 ÷ ...... = ...... people

> 150 is the lower quartile so you need to find 25% of 80.

**(2 marks)**

(c) What percentage of people have heights between 150 cm and 175 cm?

Percentage of people with height between 150 cm and 175 cm = ......%

**(1 mark)**

# Histograms

1   A survey has been conducted on how many hours of homework some children did last week.

(a)   Complete the table below.

> Frequency density = frequency ÷ class width.

| Hours spent doing homework (h) | Frequency | Frequency density |
|---|---|---|
| $0 \leqslant h \leqslant 2$ | 5 | 5 ÷ 2 = 2.5 |
| $2 < h \leqslant 4$ | 12 | 12 ÷ 2 = ...... |
| $4 < h \leqslant 5$ | 24 | 24 ÷ ...... = ...... |
| $5 < h \leqslant 10$ | 10 | ...... ÷ 5 = ...... |
| $10 < h \leqslant 20$ | 1 | ...... ÷ ...... = ...... |

**(3 marks)**

(b)   Draw a histogram to represent the information collected.

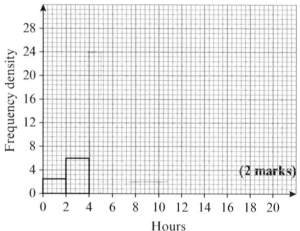

**(2 marks)**

2   The histogram represents the spread of marks (m), students achieved in a test.

(a)   Use the information in the histogram to complete the table below.

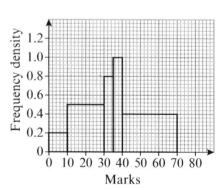

> The area of each bar represents the frequency.

| Marks (m) | Frequency | Frequency density |
|---|---|---|
| $0 \leqslant m \leqslant 10$ | 0.2 × 10 = ...... | 0.2 |
| $10 < m \leqslant 30$ | 0.5 × 20 = ...... | 0.5 |
| $30 < m \leqslant 35$ | ...... × 5 = ...... | ...... |
| $35 < m \leqslant 40$ | ...... × ...... = ...... | 1 |
| $40 < m \leqslant 70$ | ...... × ...... = ...... | ...... |

**(3 marks)**

(b)   How many students were surveyed?

............   **(1 mark)**

# Frequency polygons

**1** The frequency table gives information about the weights ($w$ kg) of 40 dogs.

| Weight (kg) | Frequency |
|---|---|
| $0 \leqslant w < 5$ | 2 |
| $5 \leqslant w < 10$ | 16 |
| $10 \leqslant w < 15$ | 10 |
| $15 \leqslant w < 20$ | 6 |
| $20 \leqslant w < 25$ | 5 |
| $25 \leqslant w < 30$ | 1 |

(a) Draw a frequency polygon to show this information.

First, plot (2.5, 2), then (7.5, 16), (12.5, ......),

(......, ......), (......, ......) and (......, ......)

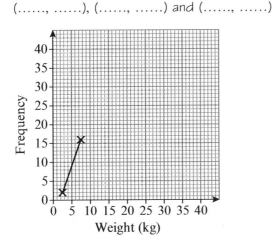

You use midpoints when plotting frequency polygons.

When you have plotted all of the points, join them together with straight lines.

**(4 marks)**

(b) Write down the modal class interval. [ Remember the mode is the most common. ]

............ **(1 mark)**

**PROBLEM SOLVED!**

**2** The frequency table gives information about the distances ($d$ km), 50 people travel to work every day.

You will need to use problem-solving skills throughout your exam – **be prepared!**

| Distance (km) | Frequency |
|---|---|
| $0 \leqslant d < 10$ | 5 |
| $10 \leqslant d < 20$ | 12 |
| $20 \leqslant d < 30$ | 18 |
| $30 \leqslant d < 40$ | 9 |
| $40 \leqslant d < 50$ | 1 |
| $50 \leqslant d < 60$ | 3 |
| $60 \leqslant d < 70$ | 0 |
| $70 \leqslant d < 80$ | 2 |

(a) Draw a frequency polygon to show this information.

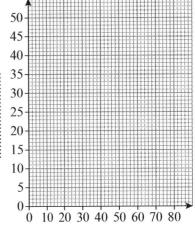

..................... **(4 marks)**

(b) Write down the modal class interval.

................. **(1 mark)**

(c) Write down the median class interval.

................. **(1 mark)**

(d) What percentage of people asked travel less than 30 km to work each day?

................. **(2 marks)**

# Comparing data

**1** The number of winning shots two tennis players have made in their last 12 sets are as follows:

Donald: 30, 21, 32, 45, 33, 37, 29, 31, 38, 38, 20, 30

Richard: 12, 17, 30, 29, 25, 32, 15, 40, 32, 25, 21, 22

Compare Donald's and Richard's winning shots

Donald's median: 20, 21, 29, 30, 30, 31, 32, 33, 37, 38, 38, 45

Median = ......

Richard's median: ......, ......, ......, ......, ......, ......,

......, ......, ......, ......, ......, ......

Median = ......

Donald's range = 45 − 20 = ......

Richard's range = ...... − ...... = ......

> When comparing two sets of data you will need to find the average (median) and the spread of the data (range).

> To find the median, order the data and then find the middle value.

> Range = largest value − smallest value.

On average, ............ is making more winning shots with a median of ............

compared to ............ with a median of ............

............ is more consistent with a range of ............ compared to ............

with a range of ............

**(4 marks)**

**2** These box plots give information about the marks students were awarded in a geography test. Two different classes, class A and class B, sat the same test.

Compare the results between class A and class B.

> Compare the median and/or range or interquartile range.

Class A

Class B

0 10 20 30 40 50 60 70 80
Marks

..................................................................................................

..................................................................................................

..................................................................................................

**(2 marks)**

# Probability

**1** A biased 6-sided dice is rolled once. The table shows the probability of rolling each number.

| Number | 1 | 2 | 3 | 4 | 5 | 6 |
|--------|------|------|------|---|------|-----|
| Probability | 0.06 | 0.04 | 0.02 | | 0.21 | 0.3 |

(a) Find the probability of rolling a 4.

P(rolling a 4) = ......      **(1 mark)**

(b) Find the probability of rolling a 1, 2 or a 6.

> Add each of the probabilities together.

P(rolling a 1) + P(rolling a 2) + P(rolling a 6)

= ...... + ...... + ...... = ......      **(2 marks)**

(c) Find the probability of rolling a 4.

> All probabilities add up to 1.

P(rolling a 4) = 1 − (0.06 + 0.04 + ...... + ...... + ......) = ......      **(2 marks)**

**2** A biased spinner is spun once. The spinner will either land on a 1, 2, 3 or 4.

| Number | 1 | 2 | 3 | 4 |
|--------|-----|---|---|-----|
| Probability | 0.1 | | | 0.1 |

The probability of landing on a 2 or 3 is in the ratio 1 : 3.

(a) Find the missing probabilities      **(2 marks)**

(b) Find the probability of landing on a 1 or a 3.      ............ **(2 marks)**

**3** There are red, yellow, green, blue and white beads in a bag. The table shows the probability of picking each coloured bead.

> You will need to use problem-solving skills throughout your exam – **be prepared!**

| Colour | Red | Yellow | Green | Blue | White |
|--------|-----|--------|-------|------|-------|
| Probability | 0.1 | 0.3 | $3x$ | $x$ | $2x$ |

(a) Calculate the value of $x$.

$0.1 + 0.3 + 3x + x + 2x = 1$

$...... + 6x = 1$

$6x = ......$

$x = ......$      **(2 marks)**

(b) Hence, or otherwise, find the missing probabilities in the table.

P(green) = 3 × ...... = ......

P(blue) = ......

P(white) = ...... × ...... = ......      **(1 mark)**

(c) Find the probability of picking a yellow or white bead.

P(yellow or white) = ................      **(2 marks)**

# Relative frequency

**1** A factory produces food cans.

The probability that a can is faulty is 0.02.

Work out an estimate for the number of faulty cans in a batch of 500 cans.

500 × 0.02 = ......                                                    **(2 marks)**

**PROBLEM SOLVED!**

**2** The probability that Owen will win a game of cards is 0.4.

If he plays 200 games, work out an estimate for the number of those games he will lose.

...... × ...... = ......

You will need to use problem-solving skills throughout your exam – **be prepared!**

Watch out! You are calculating the probability he will lose, not win.                  **(2 marks)**

**Guided**

**3** Isha orders a box of food cans.

The table shows the number of each can in the box.

| Type of Can | Soup | Beans | Peaches | Peas |
|---|---|---|---|---|
| No. of cans | 25 | 41 | 32 | 11 |

A can is chosen at random from the box.

(a) Work out the probability Isha picks a can of soup.

P(soup) = ......                                                      **(2 marks)**

(b) Work out the probability Isha picks a can of peaches or beans.

P(peaches or beans) = ......                                          **(2 marks)**

**4** There are four netball teams in a league. The table below shows the probability each netball team has of winning a match.

| Netball team | Tornadoes | Rockets | Hurricanes | Fireballs |
|---|---|---|---|---|
| Probability | 0.03 | | 0.25 | 0.12 |

(a) Work out the probability Rockets will win a match.

P(Rockets win) = 1 − (0.03 + ...... + ......) = ......

Probabilities always add up to one.                                  **(2 marks)**

(b) If each netball team plays 96 matches in a season, work out an estimate for the number of these games Hurricanes will win.

...... × 0.25 = ......                                                **(2 marks)**

# Venn diagrams

**1** A group of 40 people were asked if they owned a dog or a cat. 20 people owned a dog, 5 people owned a cat and 3 people owned both.

(a) Complete the Venn diagram.

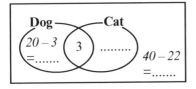

Dog — Cat
$20 - 3$
$=\ldots\ldots$    3    $\ldots\ldots$    $40 - 22$
$=\ldots\ldots$

> Always start by filling the middle of the Venn diagram first and work your way out.

**(3 marks)**

(b) A person is picked at random. Find the probability that:

> Don't forget to calculate how many people owned neither a cat nor a dog. This goes inside the box outside the circles.

(i) they own a dog only

$P(\text{dog only}) = \dfrac{\ldots\ldots}{40}$

**(1 mark)**

> Add all the answers inside the circles together.

(ii) they own a dog or a cat or both

$P(\text{dog or cat or both}) = \dfrac{\ldots\ldots + \ldots\ldots + \ldots\ldots}{40} = \dfrac{\ldots\ldots}{40}$

**(2 marks)**

(iii) they own neither a cat nor a dog.

$P(\text{neither cat nor a dog}) = \dfrac{\ldots\ldots}{40}$

> This is your answer in the box on the outside of the circles.

**(1 mark)**

**2** The Venn diagram shows 30 pupils who study history (H) and geography (G).

Find:

(a) P(H)

$P(H) = \dfrac{13 + \ldots\ldots}{30} = \dfrac{\ldots\ldots}{30}$

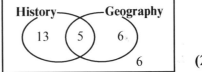

History — Geography
13    5    6
6

**(2 marks)**

(b) $P(H \cap G)$

$P(H \cap G) = \dfrac{\ldots\ldots}{30}$

> This is the intersection of pupils who study history and geography.

**(1 mark)**

(c) $P(G')$

$P(G') = \dfrac{\ldots\ldots + \ldots\ldots}{30} = \dfrac{\ldots\ldots}{30}$    These are the pupils who do not study geography.

**(2 marks)**

(d) $P(H \cup G)$

$P(H \cup G) = \dfrac{\ldots\ldots + \ldots\ldots + \ldots\ldots}{30} = \dfrac{\ldots\ldots}{30}$

> These are the pupils who study history or geography or both.

**(2 marks)**

**3** A and B are two events. P(A) = 0.7, $P(A \cap B) = 0.2$ and $P(A \cup B) = 0.8$.

Find:

> Draw a Venn diagram before trying to answer these questions.

> You will need to use problem-solving skills throughout your exam – **be prepared!**

(a) P(B) = ................

**(2 marks)**

(b) $P(A' \cup B') = $ ................

**(2 marks)**

(c) $P(A' \cap B) = $ ................

**(2 marks)**

# Conditional probability

**1** The Venn diagram shows information about the types of book read by 40 people.

One person is picked at random.

Horror ⎯⎯ Romance

9   8   16

7

(a) Find the probability this person reads horror.

P(reads horror) = $\frac{\ldots}{40}$

**(1 mark)**

(b) Find the probability that this person reads romance, given that they also read horror.

> Whenever you see the word 'given' in a probability question, this will link to conditional probability.

P(reads romance given they read horror)
= $\frac{\ldots}{17}$

> This is the intersection of people reading romance and horror out of a total of people reading horror.

**(2 marks)**

(c) Find the probability that this person reads both types of book, given they read at least one type of book.

P(reads both types given reads at least one type) = $\frac{\ldots}{33}$

> This is the intersection of people reading romance and horror out of a total of all the people who read romance or horror or both.

**(2 marks)**

**Guided**

**PROBLEM SOLVED!**

**2** The Venn diagram shows information about the sports 100 people play.

One person is picked at random.

> You will need to use problem-solving skills throughout your exam – **be prepared!**

Football ⎯⎯ Rugby

10   3   20
   10  9  12
     16     20
   Cricket

(a) What is the probability this person plays rugby?

.................................................................

**(2 marks)**

(b) What is the probability that this person plays cricket given they already play rugby?

.................................................................

**(2 marks)**

**3** The two-way table gives information about the number of pupils in certain A-level classes.

A pupil is picked at random.

|        | French | Maths | Art |
|--------|--------|-------|-----|
| Female | 21     | 13    | 2   |
| Male   | 32     | 13    | 19  |

(a) Work out the probability that this pupil studies maths, given they are male.

Number of males = 32 + 13 + ...... = ......

Number of males studying maths = ......

P(study maths given male) = $\frac{\ldots}{\ldots}$

**(2 marks)**

(b) Work out the probability this pupil studies French or art, given they are female.

Number of females = 21 + ...... + ...... = ......

Number of females studying French or art = ...... + 2 = ......

P(study French or art given female) = $\frac{\ldots}{\ldots}$

**(2 marks)**

# Tree diagrams

**1** A GCSE group has 14 boys and 18 girls.

2 students are selected at random from this group.

(a) Complete the tree diagram for this information.

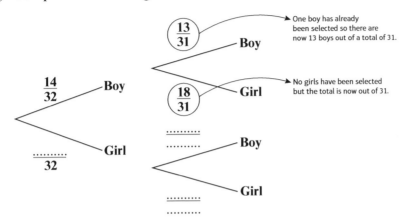

One boy has already been selected so there are now 13 boys out of a total of 31.

No girls have been selected but the total is now out of 31.

**(2 marks)**

(b) Find the probability that the students selected are:

(i) two boys

$$P(\text{two boys}) = \frac{14}{32} \times \frac{\dots}{\dots} = \frac{\dots}{\dots}$$

Multiply along the branches.

**(2 marks)**

(ii) one boy and one girl.

$$P(\text{one boy and one girl}) = \frac{14}{32} \times \frac{\dots}{\dots} + \frac{\dots}{32} \times \frac{\dots}{\dots} = \frac{\dots}{\dots}$$

Here there are two options. You can either select a boy and then a girl or vice versa. Multiply along each branch and then add your answers together.

**(3 marks)**

(c) Find the probability that the second student selected is a girl, given that the first student selected was a girl.

$$P(\text{second girl given first girl}) = \frac{\dots}{31}$$

This probability can be taken straight from the tree diagram.

**(1 mark)**

**2** The probability it will rain on Saturday is 0.2.

If it does not rain on Saturday then the probability it will rain on Sunday is 0.55.

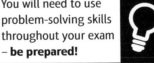

You will need to use problem-solving skills throughout your exam – **be prepared!**

If it does rain on Saturday then the probability it will not rain on Sunday is 0.3.

Find the probability that:

Draw a tree diagram before trying to answer these questions.

(a) it will not rain on both Saturday and Sunday

............ **(2 marks)**

(b) it will rain on one of the days but not the other.

............ **(3 marks)**

# Problem-solving practice 1

**1** Billy records the time it takes him to drive to work in the morning.

The results are in the table.

| Time in minutes, $t$ | $15 < t \leqslant 20$ | $20 < t \leqslant 25$ | $25 < t \leqslant 30$ | $30 < t \leqslant 40$ | $40 < t \leqslant 60$ |
|---|---|---|---|---|---|
| Frequency | 5 | 40 | 51 | 26 | 8 |

(a) Billy needs to be at work by 8:15 am. If he leaves home at 7:50 am, what percentage of times would he expect to be late?

Frequency of being late = ...... + ...... + ...... = ......

Percentage of times being late = $\frac{......}{......} \times 100 = ......\%$

> To be late, the time of his journey must be over 25 minutes.

**(2 marks)**

(b) If he leaves 5 minutes earlier, what percentage of times would he expect to be late?

Frequency of being late = ...... + ...... = ......

Percentage of times being late = $\frac{......}{......} \times 100 = ......\%$

> To be late now, the time of his journey must be over 30 minutes.

**(2 marks)**

**Guided**

**2** Three positive integers are written down.

Given that the median is 7, the mean is 5 and the range of the numbers is 6, find the numbers.

......, ......, ...... **(3 marks)**

**Guided**

**3** Lucy's Coffee Shop sells coffee, tea and hot chocolate. On Saturday, 250 hot drinks were served. 145 were served to men, 75 of these were coffee. 20 teas were sold to women and 42 teas were sold in total. 80 hot chocolates were sold.
How many coffees were served to women?

> Use a 2-way table.

............ **(3 marks)**

# Problem-solving practice 2

**4** There are 20 red and green counters in a bag.

There are 12 green and 8 red counters.

Rachel picks two counters from the bag without replacing them.

(a) Draw a tree diagram to represent this information.

**(2 marks)**

(b) Calculate the probability Rachel picks two green counters.

............    **(2 marks)**

(c) Calculate the probability Rachel picks two different colours.

............    **(3 marks)**

**5** 100 people were asked to choose their favourite flavour, A, B or both. 26 people chose flavour A, 52 people chose flavour B and 20 people chose neither.

A person is picked at random.

Find the value of $x$ and, hence, calculate the probability of this person picking both flavours.

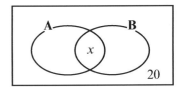

............    **(4 marks)**

**6** Two tour companies A and B asked holiday makers to rate their tours.

The information is represented by the box plot.

Which tour would you choose to go on? Give reasons for your answer.

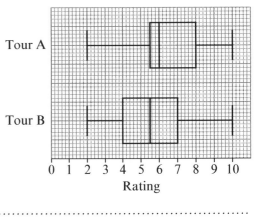

.................................................................

.................................................................

.................................................................

.................................................................

.................................................................

**(2 marks)**

129

# Paper 1

## Practice exam paper

**Higher Tier**
Time: 1 hour 30 minutes
Calculators must not be used
Diagrams are **NOT** accurately drawn,
unless otherwise indicated.
You must **show all your working out**.

1 Expand and simplify $(2t + 5)(t + 3)$

$7t^2 + 8t + 15$ **(2 marks)**

2 Write down all the factor pairs of $x^2y^2$.

.................

.................

.................

................. **(2 marks)**

3 Make $u$ the subject of this formula.

$$s = \frac{1}{2}(u + v)t$$

................. **(2 marks)**

4 Work out $7.32 \times 4.8$. Give your answer in standard form.

$7.32 \times 4.8$

................. **(3 marks)**

5 (a) Simplify the inequalities $10 + 2x > 6$ and $x + 3 > 7 - y$.

$x < 5$

$2 \times 2 \times 3$ )

................. **(2 marks)**

(b) Draw a sketch map to show the region bounded by these inequalities and the $x$-axis.

................. **(2 marks)**

130

**6** Here are the first four patterns in a sequence. The patterns are made from regular hexagons and equilateral triangles.

(a) Write down an expression for the number of triangles in the $n$th term of the sequence.

.................. **(1 mark)**

(b) Use your answer to calculate how many hexagons are in the pattern that contains 91 triangles.

.................. **(1 mark)**

**7** $a = 48$ and $b = 54$

(a) Work out the highest common factor of $a$ and $b$.

.................. **(1 mark)**

(b) The organiser of a concert wants to arrange chairs like this, either side of the walk-way.

There must be the same number of rows in each block and as many rows as possible because the hall is narrow. Write down how many columns of chairs will be in each block.

Block $a$ ..................

Block $b$ .................. **(2 marks)**

**8** (a) Work out the value of $0.0081^{\frac{1}{4}}$

$\sqrt[4]{81} = 3 \times 10^{-3}$

$3$

.................. **(2 marks)**

(b) Work out the value of $\left(\dfrac{-5\sqrt{5}}{8}\right)^{\frac{-1}{3}}$

$\overline{2}$

.................. **(3 marks)**

131

**9** Force = pressure × area

Find the pressure exerted by a force of 800 Newtons on an area of 50 cm². Give your answer in Newtons/m².

.................. **(2 marks)**

**10** The plan, front elevation and side elevation of a monument are shown.

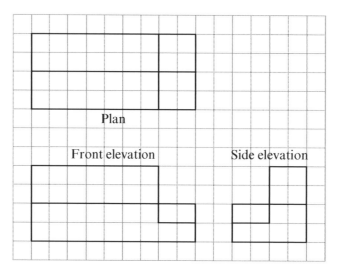

Draw a 3D sketch of the monument.

**(2 marks)**

**11** A school of 800 students will be creating a garden area for Make your School Greener Week.

Mrs Lloyd is ordering packets of seeds for the students to plant. Each student will plant one packet of seeds.

Mrs Lloyd takes a sample of 40 students. She asks each student to choose the kind of seeds they would most like to plant.

The table shows her results.

| Seeds preference | Number of students |
|---|---|
| Bee-friendly plants | 7 |
| Herbs | 11 |
| Wild flowers | 14 |
| Garden flowers | 8 |

(a) Work out how many packs of wild flower seeds Mrs Lloyd should order.

.................. **(1 mark)**

(b) Work out how many more packs of herb seeds than bee-friendly seeds she should order.

.................. **(1 mark)**

**12** The speed-time graph shows a 10-minute cycle ride.

Write down what was happening between the 3rd and the 8th minute.

................................................................................ **(2 marks)**

**13** Karina travelled by train from Newcastle upon Tyne to Doncaster. The journey took 1.5 hours at an average speed of 72 mph.

Wayne did the same journey by car. By road, the distance was 12 miles longer. Wayne's average speed was 40 mph.

(a) How much longer did Wayne's journey take?

.................. **(3 marks)**

(b) Using your answer to (a), write a ratio showing the time taken by Karina compared with the time taken by Wayne.

.................. **(1 mark)**

(c) Wayne travelled by car to save money. His car does 12 miles to a litre of petrol, and petrol costs £1.30 per litre. If Karina's train ticket cost £18, how much money did Wayne save?

.................. **(2 marks)**

**14** $y = x^2 - 4x + 4$

   (a) Using factorisation, find the value of $x$ when $y = 0$.

                                                                    ................. **(2 marks)**

   (b) Sketch the graph of this function.

                                                                    ................. **(3 marks)**

**15** In a company of 400 employees, $\frac{7}{8}$ of the staff are qualified engineers and the rest are not.

   (a) The company has a wages budget for non-engineers of £750,000 per year. Work out the mean yearly wage of a non-engineer.

                                                                   ................. **(2 marks)**

   (b) The mean yearly wages of a non-engineer and an engineer are in a ratio of 1 : 2.

       Calculate the wages budget per year for engineers in this company. You must show your working.

                                                                   ................. **(2 marks)**

   (c) Write down a ratio to show the portion of the wages budget that is spent on engineers, compared with non-engineers.

                                                                     ................. **(1 mark)**

**16** Terence has two rectangles of recycled wood. He splits them as shown and makes a square wooden picture frame with a square space for the picture.

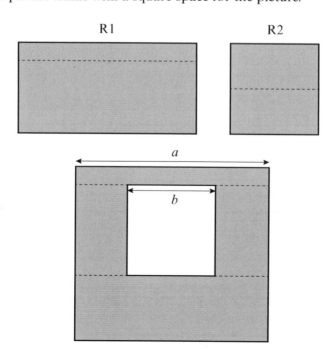

(a)  Write an expression to describe the shaded area of the picture frame.

.................  **(1 mark)**

(b)  Write expressions in *a* and *b* to describe the areas of each of the two original large rectangles R1 and R2.

You must show your working.

.................

.................  **(2 marks)**

**17** Serena is playing a board game with her brother Ben. You throw two dice on each turn.

Often when Serena is on the square marked 'Go' she rolls 7 and must move to a square where she pays Ben £100.

(a)  Work out the probability of Serena rolling 7 when she is on the 'Go' square.

Give your answer as a fraction in its simplest form. You must show your working.

.................  **(2 marks)**

(b)  Sometimes Serena rolls 8 and lands on a square where she has to pay Ben £60.

Write down the probability of Serena rolling **either** a 7 or an 8 when she is on 'Go'.

Give your answer as a fraction in its simplest form.

.................  **(2 marks)**

**18** Toni's Grandma keeps balls of knitting wool in a bag. There are 5 yellow balls, 3 blue balls and 12 grey balls. Toni takes out a ball at random. She then takes out another ball at random.

(a)  Work out the probability that the first ball is either yellow or blue.

Give your answer *a* as a decimal in the range 0 < *a* < 1.

*a* = .................  **(1 mark)**

(b)  Work out the probability that one ball is yellow and the other is blue.

Give your answer as a fraction in its simplest form. You must show your working.

*a* = .................  **(2 marks)**

**19** Ollie has designed this greetings card on his computer. It is 10 cm wide and 16 cm tall when printed.

16 cm

10 cm

Ollie also decides to print the card smaller as a gift tag. It will be $\frac{1}{x}$ the width and $\frac{1}{x}$ the height, where $x$ is an integer.

(a) Write the ratio comparing the rectangular backgrounds of the large card and the gift tag.

.................. **(1 mark)**

(b) Write down the width of the small gift tag if $x = 4$.

.................. **(1 mark)**

(c) The star on the large card has an area of 50 cm². If $x = 5$, work out the area of the star on the gift tag.

.................. **(2 marks)**

(d) Give two facts about the type of transformation that turns the large card into the gift tag.

..................

.................. **(2 marks)**

**20** Here is an isosceles triangle used to make the end of a chocolate box.

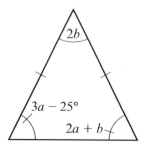

Work out the values of $a$ and $b$.

$a = $ ..................

$b = $ .................. **(4 marks)**

**21** Mikhail agrees to rebuild a stone wall for a fixed fee of £96. He hopes he will earn £24 per hour for this work. However, the job is difficult and takes much longer.

The graph shows Mikhail's time (*t*) plotted against the rate of pay per hour that he will earn depending on the length of time the job takes (*p*).

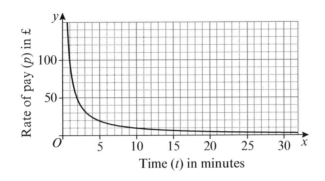

(a) Use the information in the question to write down the equation of the graph.

.................. **(2 marks)**

(b) If the job takes 12 hours, how much will Mikhail earn per hour? Use the graph to give an estimate to the nearest pound.

£ = .................. **(2 marks)**

(c) If Mikhail wanted to earn around £32 per hour, how quickly would he need to be able to do the job? Show your working on the graph and give your answer in whole hours.

.................. **(1 mark)**

**22** The diagram shows construction lines for a metal trapezium to be used in electronics products.

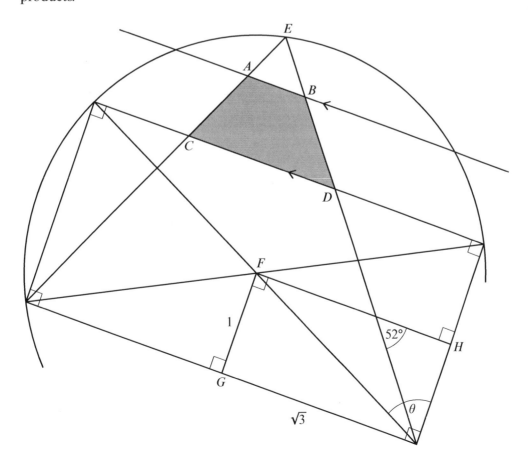

(a) Calculate the four angles of the trapezium *ABCD*. You must show all your working.

.................

.................

.................

................. **(7 marks)**

(b) From the information given in the diagram, state which one of the following correctly describes the length *CD*:

**variable**          **constant**          **integer**          $\sqrt{3}$

................. **(1 mark)**

---

**TOTAL FOR PAPER: 80 MARKS**

---

**Practice exam papers for Paper 2 and Paper 3 are available to download free from the Pearson website. Scan this QR code or visit http://activetea.ch/1GYGg8W.**

138

# Answers

## NUMBER

### 1. Factors and primes
1  (a)  4  (b)  2 or 5  (c)  12  (d)  5
2  (a)  $90 = 3^2 \times 2 \times 5$  (b)  $120 = 2^3 \times 3 \times 5$
3  HCF = 30  LCM = 360
4  HCF = 12  LCM = 240

### 2. Indices 1
1  (a)  $3^4$  (b)  3  (c)  $3^2$  (d)  $3^{-\frac{1}{12}}$
2  (a)  (i) $x^8$  (ii) $x^9$  (b)  (i) $x^4$  (ii) $x^6$  (c)  (i) $x^8$  (ii) $x^{15}$
3  (a)  $16x^{12}$  (b)  $27x^{15}$
4  (a)  $4p^2q$  (b)  $\frac{1}{5}a^2b$
5  $k = 2$
6  (a)  $6x^3y^7$  (b)  $15a^5b^5$

### 3. Indices 2
7  (a)  1  (b)  5  (c)  $\frac{1}{5}$
8  (a)  $3x^4$  (b)  $2x^3$
9  (a)  27  (b)  125  (c)  $\frac{1}{4}$
   (d)  $\frac{1}{64}$  (e)  9
10  (a)  $2^8$  (b)  $2^3 \times 3^3$  (c)  $2^4 \times 3 \times 11$
11  (a)  189  (b)  $9x^2$
    (c)  $\frac{3}{7}x^2$  (d)  $2.3 = 6$

### 4. Calculator skills 1
1  0.343 75
2  20.8
3  £98.91
4  (a)  10 950 Baht  (b)  £11.99
5  (a)  34.281 974 87  (b)  34.28
   (c)  34.3
6  (a)  0.088 427 527 87  (b)  0.09
   (c)  0.0884

### 5. Fractions
1  $1\frac{4}{15}$  2  $2\frac{5}{12}$
3  $1\frac{1}{6}$  4  $1\frac{1}{6}$
5  (a)  $\frac{x}{2}$  (b)  $\frac{2a^2}{15}$  (c)  $\frac{4}{5}b$
6  $9\frac{1}{13}$, 10 cans  7  £40

### 6. Decimals
1  0.3  0.305  $\frac{1}{3}$  $\frac{3}{8}$  38%
2  (a)  210.8  (b)  2108  (c)  2.108
3  (a)  221.4  (b)  22140  (c)  270
4  179.28
5  £570

### 7. Estimation
1  $90 \times 3 = 270$  2  $\frac{80}{8 \times 5} = 2$
3  $\frac{500}{2 \times 5} = 50$  4  $\frac{2 \times 30}{0.2} = 300$
5  $\frac{4^2}{0.5} = 32$  6  $\frac{200 \times 5}{0.2} = 5000$
7  $70\,000 \times 40 = £2\,800\,000$  8  $\frac{20}{4} = £22.50$

### 8. Standard form
1  (a)  $2.15 \times 10^{-6}$  (b)  $3.12 \times 10^4$
   (c)  $3.05 \times 10^{-5}$  (d)  $7.2 \times 10^3$
2  (a)  23 000  (b)  0.006 15
   (c)  1 315 000  (d)  0.000 901 2
3  $5.7 \times 10^0$ (2 s.f.)  4  $3.1 \times 10^{-2}$ (2 s.f.)

### 9. Recurring decimals
1  $x = \frac{4}{9}$  2  $x = \frac{25}{99}$
3  $x = \frac{10}{33}$
4  $x = \frac{141}{990} = \frac{47}{330}$, so $x + 3 = 3\frac{47}{330}$
5  $x = \frac{741}{999}$

6
$$\text{Let } x = 0.2\dot{1}\dot{5} = 0.21515151515\ldots$$
$$1000x = 215.1515151515\ldots$$
$$10x = 2.151515151515\ldots$$
$$1000x - 10x = 213$$
$$990x = 213$$
$$x = \frac{213}{990} = \frac{213 \div 3}{990 \div 3}$$
$$= \frac{71}{330}$$
7  $x = 1$ – a nice example.

### 10. Upper and lower bounds
1  (a)  9.5 kg  (b)  10.5 kg  (c)  42 kg
2  (a)  176.35 mm
   (b)  176.25 mm
3  (a)  152.5 mm, 10.75 mm, 151.5 mm, 10.65 mm
   (b)  326.5 cm
4  $x = \frac{141.5}{2.45} = 57.6$ km/h (1 d.p.)
5  $x = 20.35^2 - 14.5 = 399.62 = 400$ (3 s.f.)

### 11. Accuracy and error
1  (a)  12.35 cm and 12.25 cm
   (b)  $12.25 \leqslant x < 12.35$
2  (a)  11.94 mm and 10.34 mm (2 d.p.) with lower bound rounded down and not up
3  (a)  530.78 and 479.27 (2 d.p.) with the lower bound rounded down and not up
   (b)  500 N (1 s.f.)
4  To remain safe we need the lower bound of the lift capacity divided by the upper bound of the weight per person which gives $\frac{745}{75} = 9.93$ which for safety we round down to the nearest person and so 9 people
5  (a)  In Pascals we have a maximum of $\frac{9.485}{0.2995^2} = 105.7$ Pa (1 d.p.), and a minimum of $\frac{9.475}{0.3005^2} = 104.9$ Pa (1 d.p.)
   (b)  100 Pa (1 s.f.)

### 12. Surds 1
1  (a)  $3\sqrt{3}$  (b)  $15\sqrt{3}$
   (c)  $3\sqrt{3}$  (d)  $20\sqrt{3}$
2  (a)  $\frac{7\sqrt{6}}{6}$  (b)  $\frac{4\sqrt{5}}{5}$  (c)  $\frac{7\sqrt{2}}{2}$
   (d)  $\frac{4\sqrt{5}}{5}$  (e)  $\frac{\sqrt{24}}{2} = \sqrt{6}$
3  $\frac{6\sqrt{2} + \sqrt{10}}{4}$  4  $\sqrt{14}$
5  $\frac{\sqrt{5}}{2}$  6  $\frac{1 + 2\sqrt{7}}{3}$

### 13. Counting strategies
1  (a)  (123), (132), (231), (312), (321), (213)
   (b)  $\frac{2}{6} = \frac{1}{3}$
2  $4 \times 3 \times 5 = 60$ choices
3  $3 \times 2 = 6$
4  (a)  Nim is correct as there are 6 choices for each digit as the choices are independent, which gives $6 \times 6 \times 6 = 216$ choices
   (b)  $N$ is the 14th letter in the alphabet so there are $6 \times 14 \times 13 = 1092$ choices
5  $12 \times 11 \times 10 \times 9 = 11\,880$ choices

### 14. Problem-solving practice 1
1  $n = -1$
2  (a)  $4.35 \times 10^9$ km  (b)  $1.2 \times 10^8$ km
3  120 seconds or 2 minutes
4  100

### 15. Problem-solving practice 2
5  (a)  Perimeter of lawn is $3.1 \times 10^3$ m
   (b)  Area of lawn is $5.76 \times 10^5$ m$^2$

**6** (a) $345 \leqslant V < 355$ and $14.5 \leqslant 1 < 15.5$
Max R = Max V/Min I = $\frac{355}{14.5}$ = 24.5 (1 d.p.) and Min
R = Min V/Max I = $\frac{345}{15.5}$ = 22.2 (1 d.p. rounded down)
(b) The Max R and Min R figures agree to 1 s.f. so R = 20 amps (1 s.f.)

**7** (a) The next two terms are $75\sqrt{5}$, 375
(b) The next two terms are $288\sqrt{3}$, 1728 (One off Ramanujan's taxi cab number!)

# ALGEBRA

## 16. Algebraic expressions

**1** (a) $4x$  (b) $2x + 3y$
**2** (a) $5x + 3y$  (b) $2a - 4b$  (c) $7p^2 - 3p$
**3** (a) $6x^2$  (b) $15x^3 y^3$  (c) $35a^3 b^7 c^3$
**4** (a) $2x^2$  (b) $\frac{4x}{5y^3}$  (c) $\frac{5y}{2x^2}$

## 17. Expanding brackets

**1** (a) $10x + 15$  (b) $6x^2 - 15x$  (c) $6a^3 - 14a^2$
**2** (a) $19x + 3$  (b) $2x - 3$  (c) $18 - 7b$
**3** (a) $x^2 + 7x + 10$  (b) $x^2 + x - 12$
(c) $2x^2 - 11x + 15$  (d) $6x^2 + 13x - 5$
**4** $2x^2 + 7x - 15$

## 18. Factorising

**1** (a) $5(2x + 3)$  (b) $6(x - 3)$
(c) $x(x - 7)$  (d) $3x(4x + 5)$
(e) $3x(3y - 4x)$  (f) $5y^2(5y + 4)$
**2** (a) $(x + 3)(x + 4)$  (b) $(x - 2)(x - 4)$
(c) $(x + 2)(x - 5)$  (d) $(x + 5)(x - 3)$
**3** (a) $(2x + 1)(x + 3)$  (b) $(3x - 5)(x + 1)$
(c) $(5x + 1)(x - 3)$
**4** (a) $(x + y)(x - y)$  (b) $(2x + 3y)(2x - 3y)$
(c) $(5a + 9)(5a - 9)$

## 19. Linear equations 1

**1** (a) $x = 4$  (b) $x = 2$
(c) $x = 2.5$  (d) $x = 1$
**2** (a) $x = 4.5$  (b) $x = 3$  (c) $x = 2$
**3** (a) $x = 1$  (b) $x = 2$
(c) $x = 3$  (d) $x = 3$

## 20. Linear equations 2

**4** (a) $x = 20$  (b) $a = 21$
**5** (a) $x = 6$  (b) $a = 18$
**6** (a) $x = 5$  (b) $x = 9$  (c) $x = -13$
**7** (a) $x = 4\,cm$
(b) $x = 20°$, so the smallest angle is $2x = 40°$

## 21. Formulae

**1** (a) $a = 5$  (b) $u = 9$  (c) $d = 6$
**2** (a) (i) $30x$
(ii) $10y$
(iii) $C = \frac{30x + 10y}{100}$
(iv) £2.30
(b) $C = \frac{35x + 45y}{100}$
**3** (a) $T = 20W + 90$  (b) 3 hrs 30 mins
**4** (a) $C = 0.12K + 76.6$
(b) £508.60

## 22. Arithmetic sequences

**1** (a) 18, 22  (b) $n$th term = $4n - 2$
**2** $n$th term = $3n - 2$
**3** (a) $n$th term = $-2n + 12$  (b) $-188$
**4** (a) $n$th term = $4n + 3$
(b) No, the sequence has odd numbers
**5** (a) 1, 4, 7, 10  (b) 178

## 23. Solving sequence problems

**1**
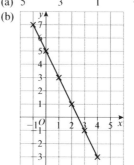
cube — 1  3  6  10  15
square — 1  1  2  3  5
triangular — 1  4  9  16  25
fibonacci — 1  8  27  64  125

**2** (a) No. The multiplier changes
(b) Yes. The multiplier is $\frac{1}{2}$
**3** (a) 55  (b) $2x + 3y$  (c) $x = 1$  $y = 3$

## 24. Quadratic sequences

**1** $T = n^2 + 2n - 3$
**2** $T = n^2 - n + 5$
**3** $T = 2n^2 - 3n + 10$

## 25. Straight-line graphs 1

**1** (a) 2  (b) $-3$  (c) $y = 2x - 3$
**2** (a) $-\frac{1}{2}$  (b) 4  (c) $y = -\frac{1}{2}x + 4$

## 26. Straight-line graphs 2

**3** (a) 5    3    1    $-3$
(b)
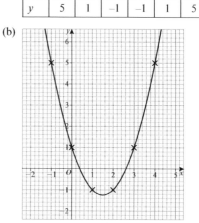
**4** (a) $\frac{2}{3}$  (b) $y = -2x + 3$
**5** (a) $\frac{1}{2}$  (b) $y = \frac{1}{2}x - 1$

## 27. Parallel and perpendicular

**1** (a) A  (b) D
**2** $y = \frac{1}{2}x + 4$
**3** (a) $(4, 5)$  (b) 2  (c) $y = -\frac{1}{2}x + 7$

## 28. Quadratic graphs

**1** (a)

| $x$ | $-1$ | 0 | 1 | 2 | 3 | 4 |
|---|---|---|---|---|---|---|
| $y$ | 5 | 1 | $-1$ | $-1$ | 1 | 5 |

(b)

(c) $-1.25$  (d) $x = 2.6$ or $0.4$
(e) $x = -0.3$ or $3.3$

## 29. Cubic and reciprocal graphs

**1** (a)

| $x$ | $-1$ | 0 | 1 | 2 | 3 | 4 |
|---|---|---|---|---|---|---|
| $y$ | 0 | 5 | 2 | $-3$ | $-4$ | 5 |

(b)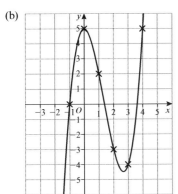

2 (a)

| $x$ | 0.5 | 1 | 2 | 4 | 5 |
|-----|-----|---|---|-----|-----|
| $y$ | 4 | 2 | 1 | 0.5 | 0.4 |

(b)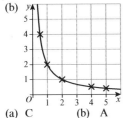

3 (a) C      (b) A
(c) D      (d) B

## 30. Real-life graphs
1 (a) £300    (b) $70\,m^2$    (c) £185
2 (a) 40 km/h

(b)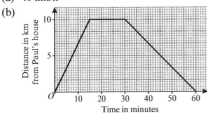

## 31. Quadratic equations
1 (a) $x = -5, -3$    (b) $x = 4, -2$    (c) $x = 1, 5$
2 (a) $x = 3, 4$    (b) $x = 3, -2$
3 (a) $x = \frac{1}{2}, -3$    (b) $x = \frac{-3}{2}, -2$
4 $x = 12$

## 32. The quadratic formula
1 $0.41, -2.41$
2 (a) $1.71, 0.29$    (b) $1.71, 0.29$
3 (a) $1.54, -0.869$    (b) $1.54, -0.869$
4 $1.35, -1.85$

## 33. Completing the square
1 $(x + 2)^2 - 6$
2 (a) $(x - 3)^2 - 8$    (b) $(3, -8)$
3 (a) $(x - 4)^2 - 1$    (b) $x = 5, x = 3$
4 $x = 2 + \sqrt{2}$ or $x = 2 - \sqrt{2}$
5 $\sqrt{2} + 3, -\sqrt{2} + 3$

## 34. Simultaneous equations 1
1 $x = 5$    $y = 1$
2 $x = -1$    $y = \frac{1}{2}$
3 A cup of tea costs 50 p and a cake costs 40 p
4 goat = £50, sheep = £35

## 35. Simultaneous equations 2
5 $x = 3, y = 1$
   $x = -1, y = -3$
6 $x = 3, y = 0$
   $x = -2, y = 5$
7 (a) From graph, intersection is given by $(x, y) = (3, 1)$
   (b) $x = 3, y = 1$, which agrees with solution from part (a)

## 36. Equation of a circle
1 (a) $x^2 + y^2 = 7$    (b) $x^2 + y^2 = 9$
   (c) $x^2 + y^2 = 3.5$
2 (a) Centre (0, 0) and radius 6.
   (b) Centre (0, 0) and radius 1.5.
3 (a) At $(-3, 4)$ and $(4, -3)$.

(b)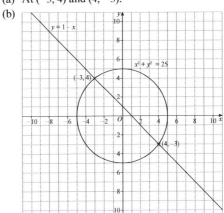

## 37. Inequalities
1 (a) $-1, 0, 1, 2, 3$    (b) $5, 6, 7, 8$
2 (a) $x > 4$    (b) $x > -4$    (c) $x \geqslant 3$
3 (a) $x \geqslant -6$    (b) $x < 5$
4 (a) $x \leqslant 8$    (b) $x \leqslant -\frac{11}{5}$, so for integer values $x \leqslant -3$
5 Ben is older than 4 years so 5 years old

## 38. Quadratic inequalities
1 (a) $-2 < x < 2$    (b) $x < -5$ and $x > 5$
   (c) $-1 \leqslant x \leqslant 1$
2 (a) $x \leqslant -2$ and $x \geqslant 5$
   (b) $-7 < x < -3$    (c) $x > 6$ and $x < 1$
3 $x \geqslant 2$ and $x \leqslant -3$

## 39. Trigonometric graphs
1 (a)

(b) Turning points are $(90°, 1)$ and $(270°, -1)$.
(c) The two answers should be close to 30° and 150°.
(d) $\sin x$ is always between 1 and $-1$.
2 (a) $x = 75.52°$ and $x = 284.48°$ (2 d.p.).
   (b) $x = 197.46°$ and $x = 342.54°$ (2 d.p.).
3 (a)

(b) At $x = 90°$ and $x = 270°$ (2 d.p.), $\tan x$ is infinite.

## 40. Transforming graphs

**1** (a)

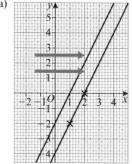

(b)

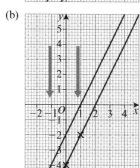

(c)

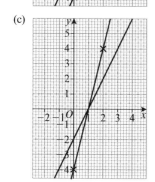

**2** (a) $(-1, 6)$      (b) $(1, 6)$
   (c) $(2, -6)$      (d) $(-2, 6)$

**3** $y = \cos(x + 45°)$

## 41. Inequalities on graphs

**1**

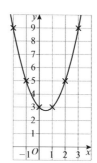

**2** (a)

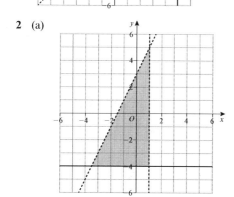

(b)

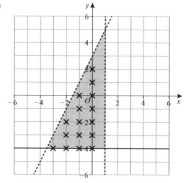

## 42. Using quadratic graphs

**1** (a)

| $x$ | $-4$ | $-3$ | $-2$ | $-1$ | $0$ | $1$ | $2$ |
|---|---|---|---|---|---|---|---|
| $x^2$ | 16 | 9 | 4 | 1 | 0 | 1 | 4 |
| $+2x$ | $-8$ | $-6$ | $-4$ | $-2$ | 0 | 0 | 4 |
| $-1$ | $-1$ | $-1$ | $-1$ | $-1$ | $-1$ | $-1$ | $-1$ |
| $y$ | 7 | 2 | $-1$ | $-2$ | $-1$ | 2 | 7 |

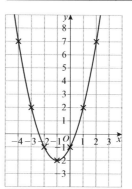

(b) $x \approx -2.7$, $x \approx 0.7$

**2** (a)

| $x$ | $-2$ | $-1$ | $0$ | $1$ | $2$ | $3$ |
|---|---|---|---|---|---|---|
| $x^2$ | 4 | 1 | 0 | 1 | 4 | 9 |
| $-x$ | 2 | 1 | 0 | $-1$ | $-2$ | $-3$ |
| $+3$ | 3 | 3 | 3 | 3 | 3 | 3 |
| $y$ | 9 | 5 | 3 | 3 | 5 | 9 |

(b) (i) $x \approx -0.5$, $x \approx 1.5$
     (ii) $x \approx -1.3$, $x \approx 2.3$
     (iii) $x \approx -1$, $x \approx 2$

## 43. Turning points

**1** (a) $(-3, -2)$    (b) $(-4, 6)$    (c) $(1, 4)$
**2** (a) $(5, -9)$    (b) $(3, 8)$
**3** (a) $(9, 39)$    (b) $(-9, 39)$    (c) $x = -9$
**4** (a) $x^2 + 4x + 9$
   (b) The vector $(-2, 5)$ translates the graphs of the two equations.

## 44. Sketching graphs

**1** (a) $(0, 4)$, $(-1, 0)$, $(-4, 0)$
   (b) $(0, 8)$, $(-2, 0)$, $(4, 0)$

**2** (a) $(0, 6)$, $(-1, 0)$, $(2, 0)$, $(3, 0)$

   (b) $(0, 0)$, $(-2, 0)$, $(5, 0)$

**3** (a) $(0, -3)$, $(-3, 0)$, $(1, 0)$

   (b) $(0, -12)$, $(-4, 0)$, $(-3, 0)$, $(1, 0)$

   (c) $(0, 0)$, $(2, 0)$, $(6, 0)$

## 45. Iteration

**1** (a) $-1.8931$ (4 d.p.)

   (b) Sequence converges to $-1.89$

**2** (a) $x^3 - 3x + 4 = 0 \Rightarrow x^3 = 3x - 4 \Rightarrow x = \sqrt[3]{3x - 4}$

   (b) $-2.195 = -2.20$ (2 d.p.)

**3** (a) $x^3 - 7x + 5 = 0 \Rightarrow x^3 = 7x - 5 \Rightarrow x = \sqrt[3]{7x - 5}$

   (b) $-0.782\,82$ (5 d.p.)

**4** (a) $0.50$ (2 d.p.)

   (b) The solution to part (a) represents the point of intersection $(\frac{1}{2}, \frac{1}{2})$ between the two graphs. The point of intersection happens when $y = x = \frac{2x^2 + 2}{5}$, so it is the smaller of the two roots of $2x^2 - 5x + 2 = 0$. The other root $x = 2$, then corresponds to the second point of intersection $(2, 2)$ of the graphs.

## 46. Rearranging formulae

**1** $a = \frac{v - u}{t}$         **2** $x = \sqrt{\frac{w}{y} + v}$

**3** $a = \frac{4 - 3b}{12 + 10b}$     **4** $f = \frac{e(1 - 4D^2)}{D^2 - 1}$

**5** $v = \frac{fu}{u - f}$

## 47. Algebraic fractions

**1** (a) $\frac{2x + 3}{4x}$      (b) $\frac{41}{10x}$

   (c) $\frac{7x - 2}{x(x + 2)}$   (d) $\frac{3x + 22}{(x - 1)(x + 4)}$

**2** (a) $\frac{5}{x + 2}$     (b) $\frac{3}{x + 7}$     (c) $\frac{6}{x - 3}$

**3** (a) $5$         (b) $2$

   (c) $18x$      (d) $\frac{x - 4}{42}$

**4** $1$

## 48. Quadratics and fractions

**1** $x = -2$ and $x = 1$      **2** $x = \frac{-1}{2}$ and $x = 3$

**3** $x = 4$ and $x = 5$        **4** $x = -2$ and $x = 3$

**5** $x = -4$ and $x = 0$

**6** $x = \frac{1}{2}(3 - \sqrt{19})$, $x = \frac{1}{2}(3 + \sqrt{19})$

## 49. Surds 2

**1** $14 + 6\sqrt{54}$    **2** $58 + 12\sqrt{6}$    **3** $53 - 2\sqrt{6}$

**4** $73 - 12\sqrt{35}$   **5** $p = 4$, $q = 8$   **6** $11 + 6\sqrt{2}$

## 50. Functions

**1** (a) $g(3) = 10$   (b) $f(5) = \frac{1}{5}$   (c) $fg(x) = \frac{1}{x^2 + 1}$

**2** (a) $gf(x) = 5x^2 + 4$  (b) $fg(2) = 14^2 = 196$

**3** (a) $g(4) = 57$     (b) $x = 6$     (c) $ff(x) = 4x - 3$

**4** (a) $x = \frac{-3}{2}$      (b) $x = 27$

## 51. Inverse functions

**1** (a) $f^{-1}(x) = \frac{x + 2}{5}$  (b) $f^{-1}(13) = 3$

**2** $(c)$, so $g^{-1}(x) = \frac{3x - 6}{4}$

**3** (a) $g^{-1}(x) = x^2 - 9$ (b) $x = \pm 3$    (c) $gf^{-1}(8) = 5$

**4** (a) $f^{-1}g^{-1}(x) = \frac{(x - 2)^2}{5}$

   (b) $gg^{-1}(x) = x$   (c) $x = \frac{5 \pm \sqrt{65}}{2} = -1.53, 6.53$ (2 d.p.)

## 52. Algebraic proof

**1** $12n + 15$

**2** $3n + 3 = 3(n + 1)$ is always divisible by 3

**3** $12n^2 + 36n + 35$ and 35 is not divisible by 12, so 12 cannot be factored out

**4** $8n^2 + 1$ is always odd for positive integer $n$

**5** $(x + 1)^2 + 1$ is always positive

**6** $(x + 2)^2 + 3$ is always positive

## 53. Exponential graphs

**1** (a)

| $x$ | $-3$ | $-2$ | $-1$ | $0$ | $1$ | $2$ |
|-----|------|------|------|-----|-----|-----|
| $y$ | $0.03\dot{7}$ | $0.\dot{1}$ | $0.\dot{3}$ | $1$ | $3$ | $9$ |

(b)

| $x$ | $-2$ | $-1$ | $0$ | $1$ | $2$ | $3$ |
|-----|------|------|-----|-----|-----|-----|
| $y$ | $9$ | $3$ | $1$ | $\frac{1}{3}$ | $\frac{1}{9}$ | $\frac{1}{27}$ |

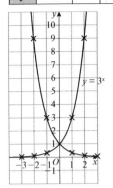

   (c) This is a reflection in the $y$-axis

**2** The graph cuts the $y$-axis at 1

**3** There are 590 people attending the fifth rugby match to 3 s.f.

**4** (a) $b = 2$    (b) Approximately 7 years

## 54. Gradients of curves

**1** $3$

**2** (a) $2$         (b) $-2$

**3** (a) $1$

   (b) $2.72$ (this is exact answer … your answers will be close to this)

   (c) The $y$-coordinates are the same as the gradient at those points

## 55. Velocity–time graphs

**1** (a) $4\,\text{m/s}^2$   (b) $-1.5\,\text{m/s}^2$  (c) $41\,\text{m}$

**2** (a) $-4\,\text{m/s}^2$   (b) $17.5\,\text{m}$

## 56. Areas under curves

**1** (a) $20$

   (b) Underestimate because all the shapes are under the curve

**2** (a) Approx. $10.33$

   (b) Overestimate as all the shapes are above the curve

   (c) You have calculated the distance in km between $h = 0$ and $h = 3$

## 57. Problem-solving practice 1

**1** $1.5\,\text{cm}$, $18.5\,\text{cm}$

**2** (a) $x^2 + x - 56 = 0$ (b) $7\,\text{cm}$

**3** $5\,\text{cm}$, $12\,\text{cm}$, $13\,\text{cm}$

## 58. Problem-solving practice 2

**4** (a)

   (b) $2\,\text{m/s}^2$      (c) $4000\,\text{m}$

**5** $x = -1.27$ and $x = -2.59$

**6** $2$ years

# RATIO & PROPORTION

## 59. Calculator skills 2

**1** $1610$    **2** £68      **3** £525    **4** £93.33

**5** (a) £20        (b) 16% decrease

**6** (a) $23.88$ (2 d.p.)  (b) £5.86 (2 d.p.)

## 60. Ratio

**1** £35, £25    **2** $80$      **3** $80\,\text{cm}$

**4** (a) 1 part = £48 ÷ 4 = 12
  3 parts = 3 × 12 = £36
  (b) £120

## 61. Proportion
**1** (a) (i) 510 g (ii) $1\frac{1}{2}$ tsp (b) (i) 525 g (ii) $1\frac{1}{2}$ tsp
**2** 18 **3** 8 days **4** £3.99

## 62. Percentage change
**1** £56 **2** £3850 **3** £102.48
**4** 1% **5** 15% **6** 15%

## 63. Reverse percentages
**1** £600 **2** £140 **3** £120 000
**4** £350 000 **5** $1.74 \times 10^8$

## 64. Growth and decay
**1** £2240.83
**2** (a) 2 million (b) 2 519 424
**3** (a) 1000 (b) 30% (c) 13 786
**4** £15 086

## 65. Speed
**1** 50 km/h **2** 140 km **3** 400 km/h
**4** 255 minutes **5** 0.5 cm/s
**6** 3.3 m/s for Chloe and 5.3 m/s for Charlie, so Charlie had the fastest average.
**7** 83 333 m/s (5 s.f.).

## 66. Density
**1** 500 grams **2** 84 cm³ **3** 2400 kg
**4** 50 grams/cm³
**5** (a) 6381 litres (b) 7500 g

## 67. Other compound measures
**1** 300 N/m² **2** 13 cm² **3** 5000 cm²
**4** 1100 N
**5** (a) 1188 N (b) $r = 12.6$ m

## 68. Proportion and graphs
**1** (a) 27 euros (b) £26
**2** (a) 10.5 cm (b) 5 inches
  (c) 15 inches (d) The conversion graph is a straight line
**3** (a) 0, 8, 16, 32, 80, 160
  (b) Line on graph (c) 31 miles (d) 256 km

## 69. Proportionality formulae
**1** (a) $y = kx$ (b) $k = 4$ (c) $y = 48$
**2** (a) $y = 84$ (b) $x = 4$
**3** (a) $w = k/z$ (b) $w = 4$
**4** $T = 220$ N **5** $d = 0.12$ mm

## 70. Harder relationships
**1** (a) $t = kp^2$ (b) $t = 48$ (c) $p = 3$
**2** $n = 16$ **3** $D = 0.24$ cm **4** 2 people

## 71. Problem-solving practice 1
**1** A: $1.085x$ so B is better
  B: $1.0927x$
**2** 86%
**3** $x \times 1.3 \times 1.2 = 1.56x$ which is a discount of 44%, not 50%
**4** 4

## 72. Problem-solving practice 2
**5** 3 km/h
**6** (a) 5% (b) £1140.23 (c) 8 years
**7** (a) 64 (b) 1728 (c) 4

# GEOMETRY & MEASURES

## 73. Angle properties
**1** $a = 75°$ $b = 105°$
**2** $x = 118°$ because angles on a straight line add up to 180°
  $y = 118°$ because alternate angles are equal
**3** $a = 30°$ because angles in a Λ add up to 180°
  $b = 30°$ because alternate angles are equal
  $c = 70°$ because angles in a Λ add up to 180°
**4** Angles in a quadrilateral add up to 360°, so angles BAD and BCD add up to 360° − 130° = 230°
  Kite is symmetrical, so Λ BCD = 115°

## 74. Solving angle problems
**1** $x = 115°$
**2** $x = 45°$ because corresponding angles are equal
  $y = 63°$ because corresponding angles are equal
  $z = 72°$ because angles in a Λ add up to 180°
**3** $x = 46°$ because alternate angles are equal
  $y = 72°$ because vertically opposite angles are equal
  $z = 62°$ because angles in a Λ add up to 180°
**4** $a = 67°$ because angles in a quadrilateral add up to 360°

## 75. Angles in polygons
**1** 24° **2** 12 **3** 144°
**4** 135° **5** 24 **6** 12
**7** 20

## 76. Pythagoras' theorem
**1** 13.0 m **2** 12.4 cm **3** 10.2 cm
**4** $BD = 5.1$ $CD = 6.2$ cm
**5** No, because $6^2 + 8^2 \neq 11^2$

## 77. Trigonometry 1
**1** 38.2° **2** 68.8° **3** 6.91 cm
**4** 345 m **5** 8.66 cm

## 78. Trigonometry 2
**6** 9.1 m **7** 17.8 cm
**8** 9.81 cm, $y = 54.9°$ **9** 74.9°

## 79. Solving trigonometry problems
**1** $h = 19.2$ cm
**2** $CD = 7.46$ m $AB = 1.9$ m
**3** $BD = 16.85$ cm Λ DBC = 33.8°
**4** 20.9°

## 80. Perimeter and area
**1** $a = 0.5$ m
  $b = 2$ m Perimeter = 26 m Area = 29.5 m²
**2** $Dx = 3$ cm $CD = 11$ cm Area = 38 cm²
**3** (a) 6 units² (b) $2\sqrt{10} + 4$

## 81. Units of area and volume
**1** 35 000 cm² **2** 27 00 000 m² **3** 1 300 000 cm³
**4** 2.5 m³
**5** (a) 7.2 cm³ (b) 21 000 mm³ (c) 3 700 000 cm³
**6** (a) 1.11 m² (b) 8 200 000 m² (c) 2530 mm²
**7** (a) 2.1 km (b) 73 m²

## 82. Prisms
**1** 540 cm³ **2** 468 cm² **3** 288 cm³
**4** Area = 120 cm² volume = 58 cm³

## 83. Circles and cylinders
**1** 38.5 cm², 22.0 cm **2** 4.0 cm
**3** 147 cm³ **4** 155 cm²
**5** volume = 19 007 cm³ surface area = 4216 cm²

## 84. Sectors of circles

1  $12.6 \text{cm}^2$
2  $4.19 \text{cm}$
3  (a)  $53.1 \text{cm}^2$  (b)  $13.3 \text{cm}$
4  (a)  $23.2 \text{cm}^2$  (b)  $20.9 \text{cm}$
5  angle = 68.8 degrees and the area of sector = $15 \text{cm}^2$

## 85. Volume of 3D shapes

1  $56.5 \text{cm}^3$  2  $34.6 \text{cm}^3$  3  $130.7 \text{cm}^3$
4  $14.8 \text{cm}$  5  $27\sqrt{3} \text{cm}^3$

## 86. Surface area

1  $144.9 \text{cm}^2$  2  $527 \text{cm}^2$
3  $318 \text{cm}^2$ (3 s.f.)  4  $119 \text{cm}^2$ (3 s.f.)

## 87. Plans and elevations

1  (a) 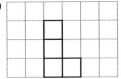  (b)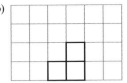

2  (a) 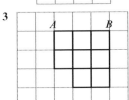  (b)  Trapezoidal prism

3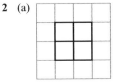

## 88. Translations, reflections and rotations

1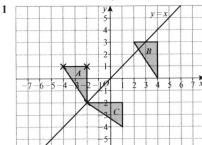

2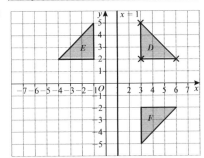

3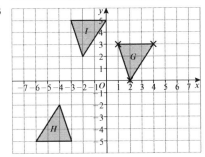

## 89. Enlargement

1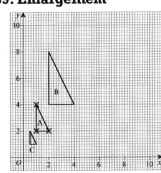

2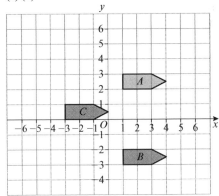

3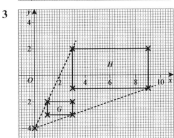

Enlargement scale factor 3, centre $(0, -4)$

## 90. Combining transformations

1  (a) (b)

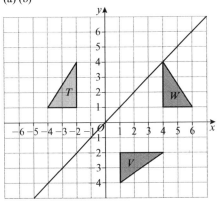

2  (a) (b)

(c)  Reflection across the line $x = 1$

145

**3** (a) Rotation 180° about (0, 0).

(b)

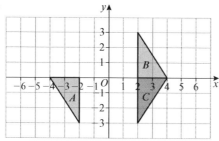

(c) Reflection across the *y*-axis.

## 91. Bearings

**1** (a) 060°      (b)   300°

**2** 290°

**3** 144°

**4** 145°

## 92. Scale drawings and maps

**1** (a) 400 cm      (b)   7.5 cm

**2** 10 km

**3** Map 1 has scale 1 cm = 6 km and map 2 has scale 1 cm = 1 km. Map 2 would more useful because if you are walking you are not going to be travelling long distances.

**4** 5 tins

## 93. Constructions 1

**1**

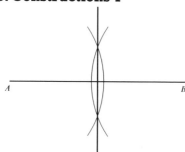

**2**

**3**

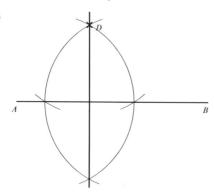

## 94. Constructions 2

**4**

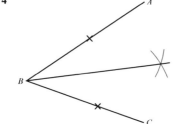

**5**

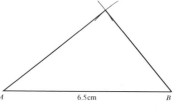

**6**

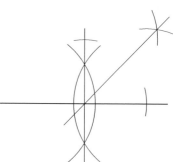

**7**

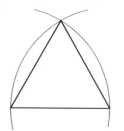

## 95. Loci

**1**

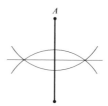

**2**

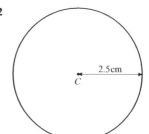

**3**

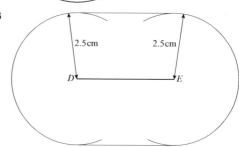

**4** Construction arc 3.5 cm from Colin's house and construction arc 5 cm from Beth's house. Where arcs cross is where supermarket could be.

## 96. Congruent triangles

**1** Answer given in Workbook.

**2** ASA

**3** (a) RHS      (b)   60 cm²

**4** SAS

## 97. Similar shapes 1

**1** (a) 24 cm      (b)   12 cm

**2** 28 cm      **3** *x* = 11.7 cm      **4** 8 cm

## 98. Similar shapes 2

**5**  $45 \text{cm}^2$

**6**  $3.0 \text{cm}^3$

**7**  (a)  $36\,906 \text{ m}^3$     (b)  $3 \text{ m}^2$

**8**  (a)  $20 \text{cm}$     (b)  $5 \text{cm}^2$

## 99. The sine rule

**1**  (a)  $11.2 \text{cm}$     (b)  $9.29 \text{cm}$

**2**  (a)  $51.5°$     (b)  $54.2°$

**3**  $101°$

## 100. The cosine rule

**1**  (a)  $3.96 \text{cm}$     (b)  $5.50 \text{km}$

**2**  (a)  $93.8°$     (b)  $147°$

**3**  $70°$

**4**  $5.7 \text{ m}$

## 101. Triangles and segments

**1**  (a)  $14.4 \text{cm}^2$     (b)  $46.1 \text{mm}^2$

**2**  (a)  $0.2 \text{cm}^2$     (b)  $4.3 \text{cm}^2$

**3**  $13 \text{ m}^2$

## 102. Pythagoras in 3D

**1**  $10.2 \text{cm}$

**2**  $7.75 \text{ m}$

**3**  (a)  $5.6 \text{cm}$     (b)  $8.13 \text{cm}$

## 103. Trigonometry in 3D

**1**  (a)  $6.3 \text{cm}$     (b)  $32.3°$

**2**  $35.1°$

**3**  (a)  $8.82 \text{km}$     (b)  $58.3°$

## 104. Circle facts

**1**  Angle $AOC = 58°$.

**2**  Angle $XOZ = 106°$. Angle $OZX = 37°$

**3**  The angle between the tangent and radius is always 90°. Therefore angle $ABO$ = angle $ACO = 90°$. $BO$ and $CO$ are both radii of the circle, which means length $BO$ = length $CO$. Draw the line $OA$. It created the two triangles $ABO$ and $ACO$. Triangles $ABO$ and $ACO$ are congruent by the $RHS$ rule, as $OBA = OCA = 90° OB + OC$ and $OA = OA$

## 105. Circle theorems

**1**  (a)  $38°$

   (b)  Because the angle in the centre is twice the angle at the circumference

**2**  31° because angles in the same segment on a circle are equal

**3**  99° (angle in the centre is twice the angle at the circumference and opposite angles of a cyclic quadrilateral ad to 180°

**4**  (a)  $81°$

   (b)  Alternate segment theorem

## 106. Vectors

**1**  $c = 3\mathbf{a}$     $d = -2\mathbf{b}$     $e = \mathbf{a} + 2\mathbf{b}$     $f = -2\mathbf{a} + 3\mathbf{b}$ or $3\mathbf{b} - 2\mathbf{a}$

**2**  (a)  $\mathbf{b} + \mathbf{a}$     (b)  $-\mathbf{a}$

   (c)  $-(\mathbf{a} + \mathbf{b})$     (d)  $-\mathbf{a} + \mathbf{b}$ or $\mathbf{b} - \mathbf{a}$

**3**  (a)  $-2\mathbf{q} + 4\mathbf{p}$ or $4\mathbf{p} - 2\mathbf{q}$     (b)  $2\mathbf{p}$

   (c)  $-2\mathbf{q} + 2\mathbf{p}$ or $2\mathbf{p} - 2\mathbf{q}$

**4**  (a)  $4\mathbf{a} + 2\mathbf{b}$     (b)  $-4\mathbf{a}$

## 107. Vector proof

**1**  (a)  (i)  $3\mathbf{b}$

      (ii)  $-3\mathbf{b} + \mathbf{a}$ or $\mathbf{a} - 3\mathbf{b}$

      (iii)  $\frac{3}{2}\mathbf{b}$

      (iv)  $\mathbf{a} + \frac{3}{2}\mathbf{b}$

   (b)  $\overrightarrow{PQ} = \frac{3}{2}\mathbf{b} - \frac{1}{2}\mathbf{a}$

      $\overrightarrow{RS} = -\frac{3}{2}\mathbf{b} + \frac{1}{2}\mathbf{a}$

      $\overrightarrow{PQ} = -\overrightarrow{RS}$ therefore parallel

**2**  (a)  $5\mathbf{b} - 6\mathbf{a}$ or $-6\mathbf{a} + 5\mathbf{b}$

**3**  (a)  $4\mathbf{a} + 2\mathbf{b}$

   (b)  $\overrightarrow{AC} = 4\mathbf{a} + 2\mathbf{b}$

      $\overrightarrow{MP} = 2\mathbf{a} + \mathbf{b}$

      $\overrightarrow{AC} = 2\overrightarrow{MP}$ therefore parallel

## 108. Problem-solving practice 1

**1**  $9°$     **2**  $6.4$ units     **3**  $2 \text{ m}$     **4**  $669$ times

## 109. Problem-solving practice 2

**5**  (a)  $2\mathbf{b} - 5\mathbf{a}$

**6**  Angle $BDE = 90°$, Angle $DBE = 5°$ and Angle $BED = 85°$ (together with appropriate reason)

**7**  Area of shaded region = area of sector − area of triangle $OBC$.

   Area of sector $= \frac{1}{2}x^2\frac{\pi}{6}$ (as $\frac{\pi}{6} = 30°$)

   Area of triangle $OBC = \frac{1}{2}BC \times$ height $= \frac{1}{2}BC \times h$

   $\frac{1}{2}BC = x\sin15°$ and $h = x\cos15°$, so area $= x^2\sin15°\cos 15° = \frac{x^2}{4}$

   Hence area of shaded region $= \frac{1}{2}x^2\frac{\pi}{6} - \frac{x^2}{4} = \frac{x^2}{4}(\frac{\pi}{3} - 1)$

# PROBABILITY & STATISTICS

## 110. Mean, median and mode

**1**  Mean 5.4     **2**  Mean 5.2

   Median 7     Median 4

   Mode 7     Mode 3

**3**  (a)  $13.1 \text{s}$     (b)  $12.7 \text{s}$     (c)  $12.3 \text{s}$

**4**  14

## 111. Frequency table averages

**1**  (a)  1     (b)  1     (c)  1.2

**2**  (a)  $20 < t <= 30$     (b)  $20 < t <= 30$

   (c)  26.2     (d)  $\frac{18}{49}$

## 112. Interquartile range

**1**  (a)  8     (b)  3, 12     (c)  9

**2**  (a)  1

   (b)  If there are extreme values, interquartile range is better

## 113. Line graphs

**1**  (a)

   (b)  7 to 8     (c)  3 to 4     (d)  29%

   (e)  Straight line on graph

   (f)  No, because the value would be over 100%

## 114. Scatter graphs

**1**  (a)

   (b)  Positive correlation     (c)  On graph     (d)  14.2cm

**2** (a)

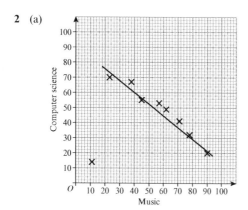

   (b) Negative correlation     (c) 40%

## 115. Sampling

1 (a) Cheaper, quicker
   (b) More accurate, unbiased
2 (a) Continuous     (b) Discrete
   (c) Continuous     (d) Discrete
3 (a) Qualitative     (b) Quantitative
   (c) Quantitative     (d) Qualitative
4 Varying the times
   Varying the days including a weekend
5 Biased means unfair. The question is phrased to get people to say 'yes'.
   Do you use your mobile phone after 9 pm?
   Yes ☐     No ☐     Sometimes ☐

## 116. Stratified sampling

1 (a) 26     (b) 9
2 777 000
3 483 000

## 117. Capture–recapture

1 (a) 500
   (b) Assumed that the sampling method used for both capture and recapture were identical.
2 450
3 105
4 6400
5 50

## 118. Cumulative frequency

1 (a) 2, 10, 28, 48, 66, 80
   (b)

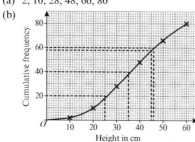

   (c) 35 cm or 36 cm    (d) $46 - 25 = 21$ cm   (e) $80 - 57 = 23$

## 119. Box plots

1 (a) 25 minutes     (b) 20 minutes     (c) 75%
2

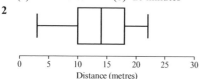

3 (a) 35 cm     (b) 20 people     (c) 50%

## 120. Histograms

1 (a) Frequency densities: 2.5, 6, 24, 2, 0.1
   (b)

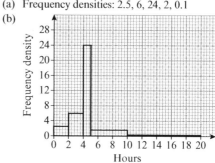

2 (a) Frequency: 2, 10, 4, 5, 12    Frequency density: 0.8, 0.4
   (b) 33

## 121. Frequency polygons

1 (a) (2.5, 2), (7.5, 16), (12.5, 10), (17.5, 6), (22.5, 5), (27.5, 1)
   (b) $5 \leqslant w < 10$
2 (a) (5, 5), (15, 12), (25, 18), (35, 9), (45, 1), (55, 3), (65, 0), (75, 2)
   (b) $20 \leqslant d < 30$    (c) $20 \leqslant d < 30$    (d) 70%

## 122. Comparing data

1 Donald: median = 31.5 and range = 25
   Richard: median = 25 and range = 28
   On average Donald scored higher and was more consistent
2 Class A: median = 40, range = 70 and IQR = 35
   Class B: median = 55, range = 60 and IQR = 20
   On average class B achieved higher test results and were more consistent

## 123. Probability

1 (a) 0.21     (b) 0.4     (c) 0.37
2 (a) P(2) = 0.2 and P(3) = 0.6     (b) 0.7
3 (a) $x = 0.1$
   (b) P(green) = 0.3, P(blue) = 0.1, P(white) = 0.2
   (c) 0.5

## 124. Relative frequency

1 10
2 120
3 (a) $\frac{25}{109}$     (b) $\frac{73}{109}$
4 (a) 0.6     (b) 24

## 125. Venn diagrams

1 (a)

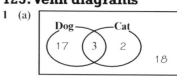

   (b) (i) $\frac{17}{40}$    (ii) $\frac{22}{40}$    (iii) $\frac{18}{40}$
2 (a) $\frac{18}{30}$    (b) $\frac{5}{30}$    (c) $\frac{19}{30}$    (d) $\frac{24}{30}$
3 (a) 0.3     (b) 0.2     (c) 0.1

## 126. Conditional probability

1 (a) $\frac{17}{40}$     (b) $\frac{8}{17}$     (c) $\frac{8}{33}$
2 (a) $\frac{44}{100}$     (b) $\frac{21}{44}$
3 (a) $\frac{13}{64}$     (b) $\frac{23}{36}$

## 127. Tree diagrams

1 (a) $\frac{18}{32}, \frac{14}{31}, \frac{17}{31},$    (b) (i) $\frac{91}{496}$  (ii) $\frac{63}{124}$   (c) $\frac{17}{31}$
2 (a) 0.36     (b) 0.5

## 128. Problem-solving practice 1

1 (a) 65%     (b) 26%
2 1, 7, 7
3 53

## 129. Problem-solving practice 2

**4** (a)

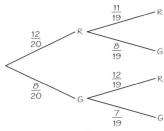

(b) $\frac{14}{95}$     (c) $\frac{48}{95}$

**5** $x = 2$ and so the probability of a person picking both flavours is $\frac{1}{50}$

**6** Tour A is better on average (higher median) and more consistent (lower IQR)

# PRACTICE PAPERS

## Practice paper 1

**1** $2t^2 + 11t + 15$

**2** $1, x^2y^2$
$x, xy^2$
$x^2, y^2$
$x^2y, y$
$xy, xy$

**3** $u = \frac{2s - tv}{t}$

**4** $3.5136 \times 10$ **or** $3.51$ (2 d.p.) $\times 10$

**5** (a) $x > -2$     $y < 4 - x$

(b)

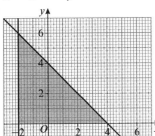

**6** (a) $2n + 1$       (b) $n = 45$

**7** (a) 6       (b) 8, 9

**8** (a) 0.3       (b) $\frac{-2\sqrt{5}}{5}$

**9** 160 000 N/$m^2$

**10**

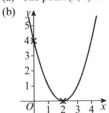

**11** (a) 280       (b) 80

**12** The cyclist was travelling at a constant speed of 6 m/s.

**13** (a) 1.5 hours    (b) 1 : 2       (c) £5

**14** (a) The point (2, 0) or $x = 2$

(b)

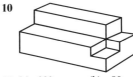

**15** (a) £15 000    (b) £10 500 000

(c) 14 : 1 (or 1 : 14 also acceptable)

**16** (a) $a^2 - b^2$     (b) $a(a - b)$ and $b(a - b)$

**17** (a) $\frac{1}{6}$       (b) $\frac{11}{36}$

**18** (a) 0.4       (b) $\frac{3}{38}$

**19** (a) $x^2 : 1$     (b) 2.5 cm

(c) 2 cm$^2$     (d) Enlargements, scale factor $\frac{1}{x}$

**20** $a = 35°$
$b = 10°$

**21** (a) $p = \frac{96}{t}$    (b) £8       (c) In 3 hours

**22** (a) $CAB = 122°$
$ABD = 128°$
$BDC = 52°$
$ACD = 68°$

(b) constant

Published by Pearson Education Limited, 80 Strand, London, WC2R 0RL.

www.pearsonschoolsandfecolleges.co.uk

Copies of official specifications for all Pearson qualifications may be found on the website: qualifications.pearson.com

Text and illustrations © Pearson Education Ltd 2018
Typeset and illustrated by York Publishing Solutions Pvt Ltd, India.
Commissioning, editorial and project management services by Haremi Ltd.
Cover illustration by Miriam Sturdee

The rights of Fiona Harris and Eleanor Jones to be identified as authors of this work has been asserted by them in accordance with the Copyright, Designs and Patents Act 1988.

First published 2018

21 20 19 18
10 9 8 7 6 5 4 3 2 1

**British Library Cataloguing in Publication Data**
A catalogue record for this book is available from the British Library

ISBN 978 1 292 21370 5

Printed in Italy by L.E.G.O.

**Notes from the publisher**
1. While the publishers have made every attempt to ensure that advice on the qualification and its assessment is accurate, the official specification and associated assessment guidance materials are the only authoritative source of information and should always be referred to for definitive guidance.
Pearson examiners have not contributed to any sections in this resource relevant to examination papers for which they have responsibility.
2. Pearson has robust editorial processes, including answer and fact checks, to ensure the accuracy of the content in this publication, and every effort is made to ensure this publication is free of errors. We are, however, only human, and occasionally errors do occur. Pearson is not liable for any misunderstandings that arise as a result of errors in this publication, but it is our priority to ensure that the content is accurate. If you spot an error, please do contact us at resourcescorrections@pearson.com so we can make sure it is corrected.

Printed in Great Britain
by Amazon